UNBROKEN

SURVIVING HUMAN TRAFFICKING

BY LURATA LYON

ISBN-9798396605343

CONTENTS

ABOUT THE AUTHOR

I am Lurata Lyon. I am a survivor of human trafficking and organ harvesting during the war in the former Yugoslavia whilst still a teenager. This experience taught me, "Being a victim is not a choice but being a survivor and a successor it's our choice".

I am now an international public speaking and presentation skills coach and motivational speaker. I have set up and run my own business in countries as far and wide as the UK and Singapore, working with C-Level clients, ambassadors and charities.

I am one of the very rare victims of sex trafficking who has survived and recovered from the psychological and physical damage inflicted on me to share my experience with the rest of the world. I believe this is a tremendous courage.

Today, I am a spokesperson for the many thousands of less fortunate men and women who have fallen victim to one of the greatest evils known to mankind.

My story reveals that the scourge of sex and human trafficking can happen to anyone – even the innocent teenage daughter of a physician living in a scenic village in Western Europe. In bravely sharing it, I am hoping to help build public awareness of this horrible evil so that it will be eradicated. Today, sex trafficking destroys the lives of millions around the world every year.

This is my story…

DEDICATION

I dedicate this book to my two heroes, UN troops from America, Brian and Peter who gave me hope and shelter during the worst period of my life. Ultimately, they restored my faith in mankind.

ACKNOWLEGEMENTS

I cannot possibly thank my parents enough for everything they have done for me, and in particular for how they acted during the worst European conflict since World War II. The decisions they took and their actions were made with the sole consideration of their only child and without any thought for their own safety. They are indeed my two real-life superheroes.

In addition, I would like to thank all of the special people who supported me in every way, during and after the conflict but for obvious reasons, I cannot mention any names. You know who you are.

Lurata Lyon

FOREWORD

U nbroken is not only a chilling account of survival amidst the horrors of war, but also a testament to the indomitable human spirit that can rise above the most unimaginable circumstances. This biography serves as a beacon of hope and inspiration, proving that even in the darkest moments, the strength and resilience of the human spirit can prevail. As you read the harrowing account of Lurata's journey, you will be transported to the heart of the former Yugoslavia conflict, where a young woman found herself trapped between the brutal forces that sought to destroy her. Lurata's incredible tale of escape, resilience, and survival will leave you both heartbroken and inspired.

In this biography, the author weaves a captivating narrative that goes beyond the headlines and exposes the brutal reality of ethnic cleansing, forced displacement, and the terrifying reality of human trafficking. Through Lurata's eyes, we bear witness to the unspeakable atrocities committed in the name of nationalism and misguided loyalty. Despite the horrors she faced, Lurata emerged from her ordeal as a symbol of strength, courage, and determination. Her story serves as a powerful reminder that even in the face of unimaginable adversity, it is possible to rebuild one's life and find a sense of purpose. As you immerse yourself in Lurata's world, you will be struck by her unwavering resolve to survive, and the compassionate and insightful portrayal of the power of hope.

This biography is a call to action – urging us to bear witness to the suffering of those who have been silenced, to honour their stories, and to work tirelessly to prevent such atrocities from happening again. As you read Lurata's story, may it inspire you to stand up against injustice, to champion the cause of those whose voices have been silenced, and to never forget the sacrifices made by those who have suffered in the shadows of humanity's darkest hours. Lurata's story is not just a testimony of survival, but also an affirmation of the human spirit's capacity to heal and find hope amidst the darkest of circumstances. Let her strength and courage serve as an inspiration to us all, as we strive to create a world where stories like hers are a thing of the past.

As an enduring inspiration, Lurata has used her harrowing experiences to become a fierce advocate for change, using her voice to empower others who have faced unimaginable adversity. Through her dedication and tireless work, she has taken on the mantle of raising awareness about the grave issues of sex trafficking and organ harvesting. By sharing her own story, Lurata has opened the doors of understanding and empathy for countless others who have faced similar ordeals. Her unwavering commitment to helping others overcome their traumas and rebuild their lives is a testament to her remarkable resilience and compassion. In addition to her advocacy, Lurata has also made significant strides in the realm of charity work. By establishing and supporting organizations that fight against the heinous crimes of sex trafficking and organ harvesting, she has mobilized resources and fostered a global community that seeks to eradicate these horrifying practices. Lurata's ongoing efforts not only provide support and solace to the victims of these crimes but also serve as a rallying cry for all of us to join her in her noble mission. Through her courage and selflessness, Lurata has transformed her own suffering into a signal of hope, illuminating a path towards a more just and compassionate world for us all.

In a serendipitous turn of events, our paths crossed one fateful evening when Lurata happened to walk into a bar just as my dear friend, Jonathan Macdonald, who knew her, was leaving. As they exchanged pleasantries, we were introduced, and it turned out we were heading to the same party. As we shared a car ride to the event, Lurata opened up to me about her harrowing past, entrusting me with the details of her extraordinary journey. Since that chance encounter, our friendship has blossomed, and I have been privileged to support Lurata in gaining the confidence to share her story with a wider audience. Despite the very real danger posed by her abductors, who continue to cast a menacing shadow over her life, Lurata's courage and determination have never wavered. Our unexpected meeting has not only forged a lasting bond between us but has also allowed me to bear witness to the incredible power of friendship and solidarity in the face of adversity.

Pete Kirtley: Award-winning writer, producer and filmmaker.

PLEASE NOTE

For the purpose of security and the safety of people still living in former Yugoslavia the names of all persons have been changed, Only Lurata's name and the names of the two American UN Peacekeepers remain the same. They are both happy to corroborate Lurata's story. All events and circumstances are based on true stories and are an accurate portrayal of the events that took place.

PROLOGUE
VELIKI TROVAC 1997

I found my parents in the basement of our house. I was so relieved. I was convinced they were dead.

"What is it?" I said. "Why are you living down here?"

I never got a reply to my question nor did I receive the sort of welcome I expected. Where was the 'Big Greek Wedding' kind of love and almost over the top drama and outpourings of affection that I had been used to? I had been held captive for many months, I had not been able to get any form of communication to them and here I was safe and sound and back home but there were no hugs and no tears of joy from my parents, no kisses or smiles. Instead my father ranted at me about how stupid I was to come back and my mother begged me to run for the hills.

"Go Lurata," my father said. "Run as fast as you can, go back to where you came from, go anywhere but get out of here."

My father continued. He said the soldiers had come looking for me many times and he'd told them I'd gone. They didn't believe him and had beaten and tortured him and abused my mother. They had returned again and again and he said he was lucky he had not been thrown in prison or worse.

"They'll be back," my mother whimpered through the tears.

Her words were instantly prophetic because as soon as she had uttered them I heard the rumble of a truck from the garden of our home and just a few seconds later the vibration from the heavy vehicle reverberated around the basement area. I heard their heavy boots on the kitchen floor above us as we sat huddled together frozen in terror. I put two and two together - someone had been watching the house. The soldiers knew the house well and they found me within minutes as they kicked and punched me up the stone steps that led upstairs. My father was trying to fight with them, begging them to leave me but he was no match for their youth and aggression as they hit him with their rifle butts. My last overriding memory was of my poor parents lying in a heap in the garden, holding onto each other with tears running down their dirty, bloodied faces. I remember being frightened and feared because of what had just happened I might never see them again. I consoled myself with a small grain of comfort that at least they hadn't been shot in front of me but I blamed myself because although my name meant 'the gift' I now knew I was not a blessing after all but surely a curse because to have this happen to you not once, but twice in your lifetime was surely the only explanation.

The soldiers took me to a warehouse and I was led to a sparsely furnished room and made to sit on a chair. A big brute of a man walked into the room. He smiled at me and for a second I thought he might listen to me, perhaps a few questions and he'd allow me to return to my parents. He walked towards me, leaned over and grinned. He then took a step back and punched me full force in the face. It felt as if I had been hit by a train as the chair catapulted backwards and I sprawled onto the hard floor.

"You are a fucking spy you bitch. We've been watching you and we know all about you. You've been to Kosovo. You've been spotted."

I dragged myself back into the chair and straining through the blood and tears made eye contact with him, mistakenly believing that if he looked into my eyes he would see the truth.

I could feel blood in my mouth and loose teeth as I begged him to listen to me.

"I'm not a spy, I was kidnapped by a Kosovan gang. I have lived in Serbia all my life. I am eighteen years old. How could I possibly be a spy?"

Between the tears I attempted to tell him the story from start to finish. I told him the truth as my father had always taught me and sincerely believed that the soldier would see that I was not lying. My thoughts drifted back to my childhood. My mother had often said that the way of truth and love always wins through and my father knew instantly when I lied and when I told the truth. He was never wrong. It's a gift all men have surely?

Not this time it seemed. The soldier punched me again and again as I begged for mercy and he kicked me all around the room. The interrogation went on for some hours and then the door opened. I was pleased to see someone else enter the room but my joy was short-lived. Two men approached me and began to tear at my clothing. They hauled my jacket off and then the second man produced some sort of metal contraption that he plugged into the wall and after just a few seconds it glowed red.

"Do you know what this is?" he asked.

I shook my head.

"The farmers use it to brand cattle," he said. "But today we will use it to extract the truth from a spy bitch… a Kosovan whore."

They were laughing at me as I begged them to believe me. The second soldier passed the branding iron to my interrogator while he lunged at me and threw me to the floor. I struggled for all I was worth but it was no good as he held his full body weight on top of me. He pulled at the belt buckle to my jeans as I tried to kick out at him. He pulled at each leg of the trousers with little effort and within a few seconds I lay on the dirty floor in just my knickers. Despite the iron contraption being more than a metre from me I could feel the intensity of the heat from it as he held it over me. I was struggling and fighting and felt two hands clamp hard on my right leg as the sensation of heat grew ever stronger and I began to tremble as my whole body began to perspire. My interrogator held the branding iron just millimetres from my calf and then pushed down hard as it came into contact with my skin. Despite the hurt and suffering I'd been through in Kosovo, nothing could have prepared me for the pain that seemed to go on and on forever. I remember screaming hard and then a misty vapour drifted up to my face. I recalled the smell of cooking meat just before I passed out.

When I regained consciousness I had been transferred to some sort of prison cell and I remember thinking that they knew I had been telling the truth but it didn't seem to matter. My cell was not so much a cell as a small broom cupboard. It was big enough to stand up but not big enough to lie down straight. There were no lights and the floor was concrete and deathly cold and I was aware of something scurrying around on the floor. And yet I was so tired, more tired than I had ever been in my life and I wanted to ignore everything around me and close my eyes. My previous period in captivity, the torture, interrogation and living constantly with the fear of death, as well as the journey from Pristina, had taken their toll and miraculously I fell asleep and sleep I did. I slept like a day-old baby.

When I awoke I wanted to go to sleep again. I wanted to believe I was in my own personal nightmare and I convinced myself that when I opened my eyes again it would all be over and I'd realise I'd been dreaming. I closed my eyes and prayed for sleep to take over me but it was a hopeless cause. I opened my eyes and as they became accustomed to what little light there was, they filled up with tears as the horror of where I was and what had happened became apparent. Pain wracked my body, my bones and muscles ached and the pain on my calf kicked in too as it throbbed and stung as if a hundred wasps had attacked me and my whole being screamed for relief from the agony I was suffering. I felt at my swollen mouth and took a sharp intake of breath as I realised some of my teeth were missing.

But the worst bit of all was when I realised I had been taken prisoner for a second time. I was in a hellhole; there was no other way to describe it, a living nightmare that wasn't going to go away. And so the only thing I could do was pray. I prayed to my God with everything I had to lift me from my dungeon hell and get me out of there.

"Please God," I whispered, "if you are testing my faith then surely I have passed. Please God get me out of here... please God take me back to my parents and let this be over."

I was crying hard and the tears dripped onto the hard concrete floor.

"Please God answer my prayers, I don't want to spend one more night in this terrible place."

Perhaps God didn't hear my prayers that day, because although I didn't know it at the time, that hellhole would be my home for six long months.

CHAPTER ONE
EARLY MEMORIES OF CONFLICT

It was 1980. I was very small, only weeks old, when we moved from a place called Skopje, now the capital of Macedonia and as a consequence remember nothing about where I was born. Looking back in the history books as I do from time to time, I figure it must have been a very nice place to live because, throughout the ages, no end of different tribes, races and people have wanted to invade and conquer what is a clearly a very pleasant part of the world. The Romans, Dardanians, Greeks, Bulgarians, Byzantines, Ottoman Turks, Austrians and the Serbs, just to name a few have all wanted to rule this part of the globe where the summers are long, hot and humid and the winters, although very cold are relatively short.

The cultural mix has always been very diverse and from as early as the 15th Century, Muslims, Orthodox Christians, Jews and Roman Catholics have resided in close proximity to each other and for the most part lived in relative harmony. And yet, looking back in those books and from the information we have at hand on the Internet these days, there always seems to be some sort of conflict in the region whether peaceful or otherwise. I don't remember leaving Skopje because of conflict and yet I now know my parents were looking for a better world for their only child, me – their daughter Lurata. My mother and father told me that my name meant *the gift* because at one point they suspected having a child was never going to happen as my poor Nani had suffered fifteen miscarriages. You are my little gift Lurata, she would tell me over and over again. Not that they used my name often, Agi (my father) would call me *ločki* which translates to darling and my Nani (mother) would call me *ciki* which was roughly the same but from a mother's perspective.

We lived in rented accommodation in Skopje and although my father was a well-respected Doctor, work always appeared difficult to come by and my early childhood was not what you might expect of a doctor's daughter. We didn't have a car or holidays to exotic places, nor were there dance classes or horse riding lessons and the other trappings of what could normally be funded from a typical GPs salary. That was because Agi was out of work more than he was in work because Nani used to say, *"He can't keep his big mouth shut, he wants to fix the world."*

Agi was what I would kindly call outspoken and very opinionated, but for all the right reasons. He thought nothing of speaking out for people's rights and freedom of expression and the right to worship whatever god they believed in or to speak any language they chose to speak in, nor was he afraid to voice those opinions in local bars and cafés and on odd occasions pick up a flag or join in a protest march no matter what the ethnicity of the majority of the marchers. If my father thought the protest was a just cause then he would be there. It wasn't altogether unusual for the marchers to be attacked by the opponents throwing sticks and rocks. On one such occasion, my father was felled by a half brick and knocked unconscious. My mother begged him to take a back seat and not to go any more. I remember my father being very subdued for some time, not very talkative and somewhat different. He still went on an odd march or protest but respected my mother's wishes and voiced most of his opinions in the local bars.

But as a result, poor Agi (and his family) suffered, as various managers of surgeries and practices dispensed with his services blaming budgets and cuts or a shortage of patients, which was never the case. My father knew exactly why he was unemployed so often, *politics* he would say, not cuts or budgets but *politics*. And although Agi became angry occasionally, not once can I recollect him complaining or sulking. He would busy himself with some job in the house. In particular, the garden, which he loved and move on, searching for a new position in the job he adored. Helping others was always my father's first consideration in everything he did whether it was in a Doctor's surgery or in the middle of a street during a protest march.

He was the strong silent type but not in a cold way and he had big dark eyes that would pull you in like a magnet. The ladies would likely describe him as handsome, with thick dark hair and rich olive skin and when he decided to tell me a funny story he would have me laughing until the tears ran down my cheeks. He never talked too much when in the company of others, especially strangers, but from an early age I realised that when he did have something to say it was always worth listening to and the tone of his voice was, and still is, like music to my ears. He was my true hero, the man I looked up to above all others and although we didn't have much I felt like the luckiest little girl in the world to have him as my father.

So when he announced one day that we were moving house, to his brother's place in a town called Veliki Trnovac, in Serbia, my mother helped him pack our meagre possessions and we were driven the short distance to our new village passing the towns of Bujkovci, Tabanovce and Nesalce and Uncle Demir met us and greeted us with a big smile at the entrance of his large farm. I was once asked to describe Uncle Demir and without hesitation, I answered 'John Wayne.' He needs no other introduction, a big strong bear of a man with a permanent smile and yet a slight air of mystery.

Those early months were full of happy memories and I discovered that my father and my uncle were building us a house, our own house just a few hundred metres away from his in the middle of town. I was so excited at the prospect of having a new house and a bedroom of my own.

I was about five or six years old at this time and life was a joy as I played with my cousins and the other children in the village and upon returning home, was showered with love by my two sets of parents, Nani and Agi and my Uncle Demir, who I called Uncle Axhi and Auntie Naxhia who I called Xhixhi. I always had the impression that Auntie Naxhia was very proud of me and never wasted an opportunity to show me off in town or to take me shopping to buy me clothes or the latest shoes. She was totally different to my mother who even to this day reminds me of a very young Elizabeth Taylor. Nani had beautiful dark hair, and brown eyes with natural long eyelashes; she was outgoing and had a smile that would warm up any room she walked into. Auntie Naxhia was almost the opposite, she always covered herself when she went out and whereas Nani always took pride in her appearance and her figure, Auntie Naxhia was always at her most comfortable pottering around the kitchen, cooking and baking. It was the perfect combination, I had two wonderful Nani's and life couldn't have been better especially when my mother got a job as a teacher at the local school. Now we had a little more money too, and there would be treats and special days out and an occasional visit to an elegant restaurant.

I didn't sense it at the time but there was a simmering tension in the house. There was nothing sinister, I think it was just a case of too many adults in one house and my uncle and auntie needed their privacy. So we moved into what was an unfinished house with no windows and no doors and still my father had no work despite his qualifications so he was unable to afford the critical repairs and refurbishment. At this time I think I first started to realise that life in general wasn't altogether fair. I had friends with doctor fathers and they lived in nice (finished) houses and their fathers had cars and worked more hours than was healthy for them. I remember questioning Agi about this but he never really gave me a straight answer. Even as a small girl, I sensed that some of the people in town and the surrounding area treated us differently, but nevertheless, we got on with life as was my parents' way, as always they made me feel I was the centre of the world. I helped Nani carry the water (we had no running water) from a well on the outskirts of town when she finished teaching. I looked forward to this daily task, treating it as a big game. We walked to the well, holding hands and talking about Nani's day at school and Agi, and what new work he was doing in the house, then we filled the plastic Jerry cans, turned around and headed back home. They were so heavy and we had to stop to rest our arms every fifty metres. It was hard work especially when there was ice on the ground and on one occasion I slipped and fell into an open drain and plunged headfirst into a metre of icy water. Nani scooped me up and wrapped me in her big warm coat and carried me all the way home.

It was mid-winter and times were hard. I remember the extreme cold and because we had no heating and no doors or windows, the wind that whistled through the house seemed to cut me in two. We slept on the floor too as there was no money for real beds until much later. It didn't matter much as I thought bedtime was great fun. Nani had made huge homemade quilts which were stuffed with old rags, clothing and small pieces of sponge and rolled away in the corner of the room during the day. At nights Agi would lay them flat on the floor and I had the job to punch out the lumps and try and make the quilts one big, flat, soft mattress, a job that I took great pride in. Looking back on those times, I realise that it must have been hard for my parents and yet Nani and Agi always had a smile or a laugh and a joke and even in those circumstances I always had a positive outlook on life and knew that things would almost certainly change. And change they did as Agi announced several weeks later he'd finally found a position in a medical practice in another village.

The only trouble was that it was several kilometres away in the mountains and by now the snow was nearly a metre deep and we had no car and he had to walk to work. I cried a lot waiting for him to return each evening especially when it was snowing hard because I remembered one of my friend's mother saying that the snow was always worse in the mountains and I convinced myself that he would fall down and never be found.

It was around this time that I first went to school and discovered that everyone was Muslim. I knew this already of course but it really hit home when I started receiving religious instruction from the Imam and the other teachers. The town of Veliki Trnovac was mostly Muslim but my early memories of practising our faith prior to school was an odd visit to the Mosque with my parents for religious festivals such as Ramadan and Eid al-Fitr. Agi didn't go to the mosque on a regular basis nor did he pray five times a day. I wouldn't describe my mother as over-religious either, for example, she never covered herself up or dressed the way some of the other Muslim women did, she was more comfortable following the latest Western fashions, a typical glamorous Turkish woman.

I loved school and studied hard and of course mother was one of the teachers. I embraced Islam and loved the religious teachings of the Quran. My first memories were of love and peace and goodwill to others and to always show respect for the elderly. It was all very spiritual and pleasantly comforting to me.

When I was a little older some of the children were learning the Quran in Arabic. I was very competitive and wanted to do likewise. When I got home I told my father what I wanted to do and he looked at me curiously and asked why. I had no other answer than to tell him I felt that it was the right thing to do. He shrugged his shoulders and said if I really wanted to learn the Quran in Arabic he wouldn't stand in my way. That was always my father's way, live and let live, say what you want to say in the language of your choosing. And so I started classes and eventually became the Imam's assistant.

With Nani at the school, I learned quickly. I absorbed the Quran studies like a sponge and enjoyed it immensely. I was near the top of the class in most subjects and was determined to be one of the best students in this new study too. I'd sit on the porch outside studying until it got too dark to see my books and then I'd lie down on a mat and watch the stars for hours. The stars and the vastness of the universe always fascinated me and I'd try to comprehend how all the stars and planets came into being. One of my teachers said that one star was the equivalent of a grain of sand on the beach and most stars that we could see were dead because the light from them took so long to reach us. Shooting stars were dying stars and I'd get a real thrill on the odd occasion I'd see one. Now and again I would see the vapour trail from a far-off   aeroplane and I'd wonder where it was going and which airport it had taken off from. I was at peace with the world lying on a padded mat watching the stars and sometimes I'd relax so much I'd fall asleep and Agi would have to carry me to bed.

But the bad news never seemed to be far away however and Nani lost her job. I remember her telling my father that she'd been asked to leave to make way for someone else. I couldn't understand this, everyone loved my mother, she was undoubtedly one of the more popular teachers in the school and many of my friends were devastated when she told them she wouldn't be teaching them again. When I asked Agi why she was no longer at the school he said something about politics and stormed out of the house. I also noticed at that time that things were changing and certain children were calling other children names and in some cases physically assaulting them. What was happening? School was such a wonderful place to be so why were these people trying to spoil it?

Even as a small girl, I was more than aware that things were changing. The atmosphere in Veliki Trnovac had changed too and although I found it difficult to describe why, it was no longer the place I'd grown up in and there was a distinctive mistrust of people but especially the authority and while I had never had a bad experience with a policeman or a soldier, whenever I saw one I wanted to turn around and run in the other direction.

I also sensed a change in my parents and walked in on many discussions where they suddenly stopped talking and I knew something wasn't right because this wasn't my parent's way. My parents were always so open with me and even at ten or eleven years old I was made to feel like an adult and very much part of anything that went on. I knew about the politics at Nani's old school and the problems in Agi's medical practice. They shared everything with me but this was so very different, not like them at all. I would lie awake in bed for many hours wondering why they were being so secretive.

I know now that they were only trying to protect me, and slowly, through the medium of television, it all started to become clear. The television news was always on in our house and the main topic of conversation and the reports and live television pictures were to do with the unrest sweeping the whole of Yugoslavia. It was around this time that Slobodan Milošević rose to become president of Serbia and federal president of Yugoslavia and for some reason, I can't explain why, whenever his picture came on television the image disturbed me and when they televised a speech he was making I had a strange desire to walk out of the room and do something else.

In one speech he said it was necessary to deter Albanian separatist unrest in the province of Kosovo. I was more than concerned because Kosovo was not that far away. It was clear from the television news that animosity between Serbs and Albanians in Kosovo was deepening by the day and in the spring of 1987 Milošević was driven into Kosovo to address a crowd of Serb. As he talked to the leadership inside the local cultural hall, demonstrators outside clashed with the local Kosovo-Albanian police force. It was clear to me even at that young age that there were many agitators on both sides and that they were spoiling for a fight.

I would be about seven at that time and that was when I really started to sit up and take notice. Not that I could avoid it, as it was becoming a daily occurrence. It started with protests and occasionally sticks and stones but it wasn't long before people began to pick up the guns. The newsmen and journalists then started to talk about massacres and ethnic cleansing and the name of Srebrenica was on everyone's lips, where it was claimed over 8000 Bosniak men and young boys had been slaughtered. It was the worst war crime committed since the Second World War they said. It seemed like the whole world was fighting but in reality, they were just the countries and autonomous regions around Veliki Trnovac and as luck would have it our beautiful town was right on the border. The Bosnian Croats were fighting as were the Bosniaks, the Bosnian Serbs, Croatians, Croatian Serbs, Kosovans, Macedonians, Montenegrins, Serbians, Slovenians, Vojvodinans and even NATO had become involved with peacekeepers on the ground and targeted bombing from the air. There were mercenaries and bandits and criminal gangs involved and of course, religion inevitably reared its head with Muslims fighting Christians, as has been the trend for sixteen hundred years. Watching the news night after night, I tried to understand who was fighting who and why, but it all appeared so complicated. Wars were normally fought between two sides but this was totally different, total chaos.

And yet it still seemed so far away. Television makes things seem so close as it brings the drama right into your living room. I wondered how far Srebrenica was. I took out a European map and found it and charted a course of exactly where it was. It was only six centimetres away but I breathed a sigh of relief as I realised it was in fact, over 400 kilometres away. I reassured myself in bed that night that the soldiers who had committed that atrocity would never make it this far.

A few months later everything would change and suddenly the war seemed a lot closer to home. I was in the local coffee bar and picked up a newspaper that someone had left. There were more tensions in the Kosovo region and the Kosovo Liberation Army had been formed, an ethnic-Albanian paramilitary organisation who were now demanding the separation of Kosovo from Yugoslavia.

For the first few years, The KLA remained fairly passive, but in early 1996 they undertook a series of attacks against police stations and Yugoslav government offices, saying that they had killed civilians as part of an ethnic cleansing campaign. Serbian authorities denounced the KLA as a terrorist organisation and increased the number of security forces in the region. This had the counter-productive effect of boosting the credibility of the KLA among the general Kosovo Albanian population. The cafés and bars were alive with tall tales coming from Kosovo and I'm sad to say that I sat and listened to most of the gossip. My friends told me what they'd overheard their parents say and one person claimed that The KLA were abducting and murdering Serbs and ethnic Albanians considered collaborators with the state.

The more I listened the more I feared the KLA. It seemed they would stop at nothing to achieve their goal but some of the rumours spread about them were ridiculous beyond belief. One young student called Arsal, claimed to know all about them and said they purchased their arms through drug running and the sale of body parts from the murders of their enemies. We couldn't help but laugh at Arsal. He was such a great storyteller. We nicknamed him Arsal the exaggerator.

* * *

My cousin's fiancé was a beautiful boy, his name was Nas and he was only eighteen with gorgeous black, wavy hair. He had been at university in Pristina, which was only an hour's drive away and most of the students from Veliki Trnovac studied there as it was the nearest university town. Because of the Kosovan unrest, the Serbian Army had introduced a curfew. No one knows why Nas was out after dark but without asking him any questions they mercilessly cut him to pieces in a hail of bullets. He was eighteen, he was far too young to die and my cousin Rejhan was inconsolable. Everyone gathered at Rejhan's house – it was the first time I'd experienced the chill of death. I stood and cried with everyone else, with Rejhan and her mother Shejnaz and the rest of the family. Rejhan's father, Sali, was in Germany working and at that point in time was in the air on an aeroplane on the way home. Nas's killing really hit home and the fear of uncertainty coursed through my body. It was all so very surreal and we even watched as the incident was reported on TV. The reporter stood where he had been gunned down and it was all too much for poor Rejhan who collapsed in a heap on the floor when the reporter walked slowly towards where the body had been found and pointed out the blood-stained road. A few hours later his broken body was brought from Pristina and we prepared for the funeral the following day.

It was the most horrible day and one that took an awful lot of energy to get through. I hadn't slept well the night before thinking about Rejhan. I wondered how she was going to cope. Nas and Rejhan were deeply in love and enjoyed a more Western courtship and engagement. Most of their friends would not have that opportunity and instead, their marriages would be arranged for them. Rejhan and Nas were different, they had fallen in love and both sets of parents hadn't stood in their way and allowed them to plan their long life together. I don't think I ever saw them without a smile on their face.

Everyone wanted to be like Nas and Rejhan.

It was autumn but quite warm for that time of year and yet I was chilled to the bone as I shivered and shook despite being wrapped up in a thick woollen cardigan. I stood in the main street of the town waiting for the funeral procession to arrive. I had been there for about twenty minutes and as the time approached more and more people poured into town. I had never witnessed so many people in one place, familiar faces but strangers too, men and women from outlying villages as well as the local people. It seemed that everyone had heard of Nas's death and wanted to pay their respects. By the time the procession came into view, the narrow street was dark with people, it was as if God had turned off the lights.

I saw Rejhan first. She was barely able to stand, propped up on either side by two women and at times she appeared to be being carried, or should I say dragged. I later found out that Rejhan had been pumped full of sedatives to get her through the day. I could hardly take my eyes off her and cried her tears with her as she sobbed uncontrollably following her fiancé's still body. As was the Muslim way, he was carried on a flat table wrapped in a white cloth. There was no coffin and his face was covered but I could clearly make out the shape of the body and it took my mind and my memories right back to when my Grandmother, Nexh, was buried when I was small. That was a ghastly day but this was a hundred times worse because of Nas's age and the violent way in which he was taken. The funeral procession passed and I slipped into the following crowd as we walked slowly through the town and towards the graveyard on the outskirts of the village.

I wasn't allowed into the graveyard, that was for men only, but I think Rejhan and her mother were allowed to pay their last respects over his grave. It was probably a good thing I wasn't there. I can't imagine what it would have been like to see that beautiful boy lowered into the cold earth.

Nas's friends were angry. He had been a student not a soldier and many of his friends talked about joining the unofficial army in Kosovo and fighting against the Serb soldiers who had killed him. It was all spiralling out of control and I feared for my village and the town's people that up to this point had escaped relatively unscathed.

It was some months after the funeral when another incident was reported on television, an incident that to me was simply unexplainable and at the same time beyond belief. Even at that point in time, with all the anti-Serb feeling in Kosovo, the young men of Kosovo still had to do a period of National Service with the Yugoslav Army that was made up predominantly of Serbs.

These poor men were sent wherever the Yugoslav Government decided to send them and in many cases they were sent to fight and restore order in places they were more than familiar with, towns and villages and cities where they had relatives and friends. I suspect a great number of them refused to fight or simply deserted and the news reported on those killed in active service. Their bodies were always sent back in coffins and the parents or families were advised not to open them because in many cases the bodies had been shot or blown to pieces. The TV was reporting on a scandal that had angered the Kosovans and in particular the Muslim population. A young serving soldier of nineteen years of age had been killed and his body returned to his parents in Pristina in a closed coffin. The authorities once again had ordered the coffin not to be opened as their son had been almost blown to bits by a land mine. The normal Muslim funeral prepares the body for burial when the family or other members of the community wash and shroud the body. The deceased is washed respectfully, with clean and scented water, in a manner similar to how Muslims make ablutions for prayer. The body is then wrapped in sheets of clean, white cloth. On this particular occasion, the mother felt she was unable to grieve properly for her son and almost as soon as the coffin came into the house she insisted on opening it and performing the pre-funeral rites. Her family advised her against such a practice but she insisted, as she wanted to wash whatever was left of her son. In the end, her protests won through and they reluctantly opened the coffin. To everyone's amazement, the body was completely intact and instead of bullet holes and shrapnel wounds, it appeared as if a surgeon had worked him on. There wasn't a single scratch on his face. Instead, it appeared that he had been cut open by someone with medical knowledge as a 'Y' shaped scar ran the length of his body from just below his neck to his groin region. The authorities could give no explanation why. He had been neatly stitched together and there was no apparent cause of death. No bullet or mine damage could be found on any part of the body. It was a scandal with huge implications but even the TV news channel refused to suggest a likely cause or indeed reason for his death. That didn't stop the Kosovan rumour mill. They claimed he had been executed and that the ratio of Kosovan soldiers dying while on National service was ridiculously high. The young men and indeed the adults were furious and there were protests and riots all over Kosovo. I'm sure there were many reprisals carried out against Serbs in revenge 'tit for tat' killings. One man interviewed on TV even suggested that the young man had been summarily executed and his organs removed for sale. I thought that comment was a little over the top. It was like something out of Mary Shelley's 'Frankenstein.'

Over the coming months the recruiters from the Kosovo Liberation Army came to Veliki Trnovac. We were right on the border between Kosovo and Serbia and it was inevitable. The Albanian-speaking young men from the town were ready to help their Albanian-speaking   brothers from Kosovo and I don't think the recruiters had too much trouble persuading the men, who saw themselves as freedom fighters, to pack their bags and make the short journey to Pristina and other areas of conflict.

The young men seemed more than happy to fight for 'the cause' and on one or two occasions as they left the town, I watched as they pumped their fists in the air, holding up guns and rifles from car windows as their friends cheered and clapped them on their way.

CHAPTER TWO
STICKS AND STONES TO BREAK
YOUR BONES

Nani and Agi were at home one evening discussing the unrest in the next town called Bujanovac. There was an Albanian-speaking school there and the Serbian authorities had informed them that the curriculum of the school would be changed overnight. The school was no longer to take lessons in Albanian and that only Serbian should be spoken. I remember thinking that wasn't so bad as everyone spoke the two languages anyway, even the children. But my parents and especially Agi was furious saying that it was a human right to be able to speak in whatever tongue they wanted and the Albanian-speaking schools had been in existence for over a hundred years.

Bujanovac was only ten minutes' drive away and was what was known as a mixed town. Serbs lived side by side with Albanian-speaking people who made up a large portion of the residents. Fifty per cent of the town were Orthodox Christian and fifty per cent Muslim. The tension at the school simmered for many weeks and the Serbian Army were often in attendance to keep control. It was said that behind closed doors the teachers continued to give lessons in Albanian but over time, gangs of young Serb men formed and began to taunt and abuse the children and teachers alike as they made their way to lessons. As the abuse and the crowds and the violence grew (while the Serb Army stood and watched) many of the teachers and the pupils stayed at home. They were genuinely too scared to walk the daily gauntlet of abuse and even the Headmaster resigned.

The school was slowly dying and it appeared there was nothing anyone could do to stop it from closing. It seemed the rule of the mob had won through in Bujanovac, that is until a document was leaked detailing that the Serbian Army would take over the premises once the last pupil and teacher had vacated the building. That seemed to galvanise the Albanian-speaking population and in particular, my parents who offered unwavering support for the school at Bujanovac.

One night Nani announced that she would take a job at the school. My father looked concerned but she was having none of it. She explained that she was a very good teacher and the school needed teachers and therefore she would apply for a position in the town and the children would be taught in the language they had always been taught in. I looked at Agi when Nani came out with this and although he certainly wasn't happy that his wife was putting herself in the line of fire, I'm sure I caught a flicker of a smile of admiration and of course, we both knew he would back her all the way. Whatever people said of my parents I did not look upon them as rebels. A little militant perhaps, but they were pacifists too and tolerant of everything and everyone with an unwavering determination that no one could change.

So some weeks later a letter arrived telling Nani she could start work at the school whenever she was ready. She was grinning broadly as she announced she would be there first thing on Monday morning. I confess, that weekend I was absolutely petrified and didn't want Monday morning to come.

By this time there were very few teachers and pupils at the school and it became known in the town that a new teacher would be joining their ranks. The mob was out in force that day including whole families who ridiculed and taunted my mother as she walked through the gates. She was having none of it as she walked towards the school gates with her head held high. As she reached the entrance of the school one or two stones were thrown and a glass bottle but the perpetrators' aim was poor and they missed their intended target. When she came out of school the mob had swelled in numbers and she noticed one or two of her old friends in their ranks too.

My father looked on proudly as Nani explained her working day over dinner that evening. She said there had only been three pupils in the class and the school had resembled a ghost town. As I sat and listened I thought my mother was fighting a losing battle and yet as she   and Agi spoke there was a determined positive vibe as we sat cross-legged around a low table eating dinner. Despite the hostility and the abuse Nani suffered there was no doubt about it… she was more than happy in what she was doing and confidant that people would eventually see sense.

As the weeks passed something strange happened. The mob became smaller and the pupil numbers grew. It appeared that Nani and the other teachers had turned the tide and Nani was all grins one evening as she announced proudly that the pupils now outnumbered the mob. The protesters and antagonizers were growing bored it seemed and had turned their anger and hostility elsewhere. One of the mothers who had stood and shouted at the teachers in the early days even came to Nani and apologised. She said that she had been caught up in something she knew very little about and now realised that the teachers wanted nothing more than to be able to teach the children.

A few days later the Serbian Army were conspicuous by their absence at the school and eventually, it returned to normal. We were all so relieved and happy and I can remember a celebration dinner of sorts when Nani came home that afternoon.

I lay on the sofa that evening and thought things through. Common sense would always prevail I whispered to myself, good would always triumph over evil. Soon these little hostilities would come to an end and we could all get back to normal.

But it didn't happen. The victory for the school at Bujanovac and for common sense was soon forgotten. We were watching more and more killings and unrest on TV and there was open fighting between Serbian forces and the Kosovo Liberation Army. Every day, every week seemed to propel us closer and closer to a Yugoslav Armageddon and massacres in towns and villages and indiscriminate killings were commonplace. It appeared there were agitators everywhere, men in particular, who looked as if they were happy for the war to continue, happy to agitate and escalate the violence. It was plainly obvious to everyone that a major Kosovo war with Serbia was inevitable.

But there was still a little hope and I reminded myself of my wonderful parents and their outlook on life and how Nani and Agi always tried to take a positive stand, no matter what was going on around us. Agi said that stabilisation forces and NATO peacekeepers were on the ground and we just had to hope and pray that people would see sense and the peacekeepers would bring about a permanent ceasefire. And while there had been some small-scale violence in Veliki Trnovac, no one had been shot on our streets.

CHAPTER THREE
A MASSACRE AVERTED

We lived in fear of murder coming to our village or even worse, a massacre of the entire population. The news on TV and the newspapers, especially those brought in from Kosovo, were covering incidents of mass killings and *ethnic cleansing*. I must have been around seventeen years of age when I first heard that term and even though I didn't actually know what it meant it made my blood run cold. I asked my father outright exactly what ethnic cleansing meant and he explained to me in detail including the stories of soldiers indiscriminately raping young girls and women. I think he guessed it was time that I should know what possible dangers lay ahead of me.

The television newsman was saying that there were too many reports of massacres for them to be without foundation and more and more *survivors* were coming forward to tell of grave incidents at places such as Tuzla, Zvornik and Visegred. It's not unfair to say that most of the massacres were reported to have been carried out by Serb soldiers and police but of course, their generals and politicians were denying everything. I wanted to believe them… sincerely I wanted to believe them all. I knew what the word propaganda meant too and I was well aware that all sides in the conflict tried to score points against their enemies to try and motivate their foot soldiers and at the same time court sympathy from the outside world, especially the European Union and NATO who were now heavily involved in the conflict. In fact, NATO was now coordinating air strikes on Serb positions in Kosovo pushing the Serb Army back to the border. At first, I believed that it was a good thing that NATO had intervened in Kosovo but my father made a chillingly accurate prediction. I can still hear his words to this day.

"It's all well and good turning the heat up but it's the towns and villages on the border that will suffer the most."

I was well aware that Veliki Trnovac was fifteen kilometres from the Kosovo border and I was also aware of an illegal army who were hiding out in the mountains close to Hodonoc, twenty kilometres away. They were made up of Albanian-speaking Kosovan's affiliated with   the KLA and many of them, mostly the young men, came from our hometown. That made Veliki Trnovac a legitimate target in the eyes of the Serbs.

It was late autumn and light flurries of snow hung in the air most evenings. We had yet to have a covering in town but we could see the snow lying on the tops of the surrounding mountains including our mountain Malë Ternovc. We were having dinner at home when we first heard the noise outside. The garden had a raised wall with steel gates that were either being climbed or forced open. Whoever was trying to get through them clearly didn't have a key. My father had run upstairs for some reason. At first, I thought it might have been to get the key to the gates, but no, he was trying to get a better look from an upstairs window. I heard the familiar sound of military boots running up the path towards the front door and before we could do anything a soldier had kicked the door from the hinges. It didn't matter to him that it had been open at the time. He wore a Serb Army Uniform with a mask that covered his face. He clearly didn't want to be identified.

"What is it?" Agi shouted from the top of the stairs. "How can we help you?"

Looking back it seemed like a silly thing to say and yet it diffused the tension for a few vital seconds. The soldier spoke in Serbian, he ordered everyone from the house and as another four of them stormed in I began to shake with fear. They were screaming at my father to come down, training their rifles on him. He obeyed and calmly walked towards them.

"How can I help you?" he repeated.

One of the soldiers lunged at him and grabbed him by the shirt collar.

"Get your wife and your pretty little daughter into the street before I put a fucking bullet into your skull," he snarled.

I remember thinking that my father was very calm but I also remember looking at one of the soldiers who clearly couldn't take his eyes off me. I felt vulnerable, more vulnerable than I had ever felt in my life and the horror stories that I'd heard about what soldiers did to young girls came flooding back. Nani and Agi were standing next to the front door where the winter coats were hanging on a hook and Agi politely asked if we would be out of the house very long. The soldier pointed to the coats indicating that we could put them on. Agi sat on the floor and reached for his boots while Nani took a coat and a scarf from the hook.

"Fucking hurry up," one of them shouted and cuffed Agi across the back of the neck. "I'll fuck your wife and daughter one after the other if you don't get a move on."

I was more shocked by their bad language than I was by their aggressive nature. I could feel the tension and menace in the air and yet bizarrely I was more upset at the filth that had poured from their mouths. These were not the sort of words ever uttered in Agi's house, at my uncle's or even in the school-yard.

As I made to walk towards the door the soldier who had been looking at me blocked my path, slid his hand around my back and grabbed my buttock. I was frozen in fear and despite the fact his face was covered I could tell he was grinning a perverted grin from ear to ear. Thankfully he released me and moved out of the way telling me to put a coat on. As I walked passed him he slapped my backside hard. I wanted to turn around and hit him but I managed to control myself. I sensed that it wouldn't take much of an excuse for these soldiers to shoot all three of us.

We were marched out of the house, through the garden and into the street then made to form part of a line of other villagers we of course recognised as our neighbours. We were ordered not to talk and as we stood in the cold my mother put her arm around me and pulled me in tight.

"What's happening Nani, what do they want with us?"

Nani didn't answer. She shook her head and placed a finger across her lips motioning that I should be quiet. We stood for some time while every single house in the town was cleared of its inhabitants. It was plain to see that the Serb soldiers had wanted everyone out of the houses and onto the street. There were children in nightclothes and the elderly with walking sticks and even heavily pregnant women who all stood in a long silent line. The only noise I could hear was of children crying and of course, the soldiers barking out their orders.

"It's cold," one man said.

He pointed to his wife who was carrying a small child in her arms.

"My daughter is only six weeks old, she needs to go home."

A soldier stepped forward and head-butted him on the bridge of the nose. There was a loud 'pop' and the man collapsed in a heap onto the ground. A few of the women screamed out but the man said nothing more.

The soldier took a step backwards.

"I said no talking."

The man was helped to his feet as his wife offered him a handkerchief to stem the flow of blood and soon afterwards we were on the march.

There were around a thousand villagers and we were tightly packed into a group overseen by about one hundred and fifty soldiers with rifles and machine guns. I clung to my mother as Agi walked alongside us. It was a slow progress as we were tightly packed together and yet the soldiers kept shouting at us telling us to hurry. One man shouted that he couldn't walk any faster and he was knocked to the ground with a rifle butt in his back. It was terrifying and I tried not to think of what was waiting for us when we got to wherever it was they were taking us. The fact that they were taking the entire village made me fear the worst. It was clear they didn't want any witnesses to whatever it was they were going to do. The names of the massacres at Gospic and Dalj and Vukovar burrowed into my brain even though I tried my hardest to blot out the images I'd seen from the TV reports.

We walked uphill and the tightness in my calf muscles was unbearable and of course, it was getting colder as we climbed ever higher. I became aware of a commotion up ahead and I recognised a familiar voice. It was my Uncle Demir who stood with my Auntie Naxhia and her little boy, my cousin Amir. It appeared Uncle Demir was refusing to move and when we saw him he had blood pouring from the corner of his eye where one of the soldiers had clearly hit him.

"I am waiting for my brother."

He was pleading with the soldier.

"Is that not too much to ask?"

The soldier was urging him forward but at that moment he spotted us.

"There he is, there he is," he shouted, "I will move now, don't worry I will move now."

This seemed to placate the soldier and as my father and Uncle Demir embraced briefly, we were on the move again. I was still holding onto my mother for dear life but homed in on my father and his brother's whispers. They were both strangely calm, unlike me, and my heart was beating so loud I was convinced the soldiers could hear it.

"What do you think is happening?" my father said.

"I fear the worst." Uncle Demir said. "It's not looking good brother."

"Shut up you mother fuckers," one of the soldiers bellowed and it was all quiet again.

I stared at the soldier who had yelled. His face was covered from the mouth down. His hair was unkempt and he was unshaven with a pockmarked face. Not the smart, well-groomed, normal-looking military type. Father had said that half the Serbian army was made up of released prisoners and mercenaries, battle-hardened vicious men, desensitised and lacking compassion.

We were walking up the main road leading through the mountains to Kosovo. The road was narrowing as it wound its way in between two mountains and I recalled picnicking there in the summertime. The grass was always greener and softer than the grass in the village and there was a waterfall too, a waterfall we'd play in and stand under until we were numb with the cold. It was an altogether different scene from the memories I had of this beautiful place. Now it was dark and grey and eerie and a few flakes of snow began to fall. The soldiers ordered us to stop and I was shaken from my pleasant thoughts. I could sense a small panic building as once again I became aware of a conversation between my father and his brother.

"Shush brother," Demir said, "you are the clever one, a doctor, but when it comes to trading and business deals I am streets ahead of you. Let me do what I must do."

My father was begging my Uncle Axhi to stay with us as was Auntie Naxhia but he was having none of it. Uncle Demir had singled out one of the soldiers and had walked straight up to him. I remember bursting into tears thinking I'd never see my uncle again and yet I listened carefully to the conversation that I could clearly make out from the stunned and silent crowd. My father had leaned against a tree and was shaking his head, tears running down his face.

"You, boss man, what's the deal here?" Uncle Axhi said.

The man was holding a walkie-talkie and I think that's why Uncle Demir had singled him out.

"There's no deal you stupid bastard, now get out of my face before I stick a knife in you."

Quick as a flash Uncle Demir responded.

"Of course there's a deal, now what is it because whatever it is I can give you more."

The man took a step forward and I feared the worst as I closed my eyes tight.

"The deal is we kill you all," he said. "Call it what you like, a massacre, ethnic cleansing, whatever, you are all going to die. That's the fucking deal."

The man hadn't attempted to lower his voice and every word was perfectly audible in the still night air. People started to panic at this point and there were whispers of bravado amongst the young men and adults but most of the people were crying, frozen in fear as they felt their worst nightmares were about to come true. The walkie-talkie burst into life and in plain Serbian the words that filtered through the airwaves chilled me to the bone.

"Do it. Do it now."

It was so loud. I think most people heard it and the panic rose to a new level as the man Uncle Demir was talking to, pulled his rifle from his shoulder.

"Wait!" Uncle Demir said. "If that's your boss tell him we have a deal. I'll pay you double whatever it is you're being paid. I have enough money to buy you all off."

The other soldiers were herding us like sheep, pushing us together in lines, pointing their guns at us and hitting or kicking anyone who failed to move quickly enough. It appeared the boss soldier wasn't listening but Uncle Demir wasn't giving up.

"They'll hunt you down and you'll be tried as war criminals. NATO never gives up and they'll get you one day."

The boss soldier was strangely curious now and it seemed Uncle Demir had no intention of quitting.

"They're still hunting Nazis to this day, is that what you want? Take my money and live in peace for the rest of your lives."

Uncle Axhi spoke at a ferocious rate talking about trials and executions at a place called Nuremburg.

"You've seen the trials on TV, the old black and white footage of the men in the dock."

"Shut the fuck up big mouth."

I fully expected the sound of a shot because Uncle Axhi wasn't slowing down but the soldier seemed to hesitate for a moment. And then he stared at my uncle and held up a hand in front of his face. My uncle stopped speaking and the soldier slung his rifle back onto his shoulder and reached for his walkie-talkie. To everyone's amazement, he relayed Uncle Demir's request to the man on the other end and he appeared to listen. There followed several minutes of intense negotiations and then my uncle walked over to us and said he was leaving. He said they had a deal and he was going home to give them everything he had. I thought he was crazy. If these men were mercenaries and ex-prisoners then they would take whatever he had and still kill him. That's what happened in every American gangster movie I'd ever watched.

"I'm going with you Demir," my mother announced.

He was shaking his head, the soldiers were shaking their heads but Nani was having none of it. I didn't want her to leave me and Agi and Auntie Naxhia didn't want her to go either, but she insisted and in the end, everyone gave in... even the soldiers. Nani had the most determined streak in her and her father often said she would get anything she wanted if she put her mind to it. Nani and Uncle Demir climbed aboard a vehicle with three or four soldiers and it disappeared into the darkness.

I buried myself into my father's coat and cried.

"Hush my child," he said. "It might just work. Don't you know your Uncle Demir is one of the richest farmers in the Balkans?"

"He is?"

"Yes."

My father nodded.

I had never been so thirsty in my life and yet it didn't make sense because it was cold, not hot and I had drank plenty of water with my evening meal. Father said it was the fear, the adrenalin. I looked at my watch. Uncle Demir and my mother had been gone for forty minutes now and I convinced myself we would never see them again. People were sitting on the ground, some looked resigned to their fate and Amir clung to my auntie as he shivered in the cold air. Even my father had become disillusioned, muttering under his breath that his brother should have stayed with his family and at least we would have all died together. That wasn't like Agi and I scolded him. He looked at me, smiled and then gently stroked my face.

I was cold and the thirst bothered me, I still didn't understand it. I looked up into the canopy of the forest, the night stars peeked through the light cloud cover and everything looked so beautiful. I thought it was a nice place to die.

An hour had passed and as each minute ticked by I sensed it had been a brave but hopeless cause that Uncle Demir had pursued. Suddenly I was startled by a scream and then another and was aware of people stirring and some starting to stand. I looked at Auntie Naxhia who had started to cry again and to my horror I noticed that the soldiers were walking towards us.

If it was possible, the mass huddle grew ever tighter as everyone pushed together trying to put distance between themselves and the soldier's guns. The boss soldier with the walkie-talkie moved to the front and spoke, or rather barked out an order.

"You will wait here twenty minutes. If you move in that twenty minutes you will be shot."

He told us he would position soldiers in the forest and down the road to Veliki Trnovac and anyone who disobeyed his instructions would be killed. Within a minute every single soldier had disappeared leaving us cold, tired and confused. No one could understand what was happening, it didn't make any sense.

"They will bomb us from the air," one man said. "They bombed a market that way and killed hundreds."

But no, that didn't make sense I thought. If they wanted to kill us then they would have to kill us all so that no one could point the finger of blame. Uncle Demir had been right, they never stopped hunting war criminals and if they tried to bomb us then everyone would scatter immediately and many people would escape the carnage no matter how accurate the bombs were.

I think we stayed there for about ten minutes and then the hysteria rose to a panic level. The wind played tricks on us and I was convinced I heard the drone of aircraft even though they never came. So slowly but surely we made our way back down the mountain.... over one thousand men, women and children from the town of Veliki Trnovac, one thousand men, women and children from babes in arms to men and women in their nineties who for nearly two hours were convinced they were about to be massacred at any minute by a Serb Army Death

Squad. I trembled with fear as I took each step, scanning the trees for the soldiers in hiding, waiting for the sound of the crack of a rifle, searing pain and then nothingness.

But there was no one in the small copses, no soldiers hiding behind bends or crouching behind garden walls. They had gone.

I knew by the time we had reached Uncle Demir's house that miraculously the soldiers had somehow kept their word. We found my uncle and my mother sitting on the garden wall. They had their head in their hands and were clearly crying. As we shouted over to them they looked up in astonishment and then the tears of pain were replaced with tears of joy and they were smiling and running towards us.

My mother was crying like a baby as she held me.

"We thought you were dead ciki, we thought you were dead," she repeated over and over again.

We found out that Nani and my uncle had been sitting on that wall for over thirty minutes and just like our neighbours at the top of the mountain, as each minute ticked by they had been convinced that the soldiers had reneged on the deal.

We watched the relieved town folk of Veliki Trnovac troop by us for several minutes, their faces painted a mixture of emotions. Yes, there were faces still lined with fear and uncertainty but on the whole, they were visibly relieved that the town of Veliki Trnovac hadn't become another statistic in this ridiculous war. After the last family had passed us by we turned and walked towards Uncle Demir's house where he promised us a warm fire and some hot drinks.

Sitting around the big wooden dining table Uncle Demir relayed everything that had happened.

"I sensed we would all be killed anyway but it was still worth a chance. I knew how much money I had and I knew it would impress the greedy bastards."

It was the first time I had heard Uncle Demir swear. No one seemed too troubled, not even my father who normally frowned on anyone who swore, especially girls.

He continued.

"I had millions of dinar locked in safes in the house and we started there. I emptied everything out but sensed it wasn't quite enough so I started digging up the gold in the garden."

"You have gold in the garden Uncle Axhi?" I asked.

He looked at me and smiled.

"Had, Lurata… I had gold in the garden."

"What did I tell you? He is the richest farmer in the Balkans," my father said.

"Correction brother," my uncle said, "I *was* the richest farmer in the Balkans."

He paused and took a drink from a steaming hot coffee cup.

"All the while I talked to them about war criminals and how there would be nowhere to hide and that the money I was about to give them would set each individual up for life, so why not enjoy it living in peace without looking over your shoulder every five minutes."

My mother interjected. She said she'd never seen so much money and gold in her life.

"I sensed I was getting through to some of the bastards and the more gold I pulled out of the ground the more of them came over to my way of thinking. Soon they were arguing amongst themselves, some were for killing us but most listened to reason."

Uncle Demir looked at my father.

"I told you I was the one when it came to talking, didn't I brother?"

My father grinned. It was so nice to see his smile again.

"You did Demir… you did. Perhaps one day they will write a book about you. It would be entitled Veliki Trnovac, the massacre that never was."

Uncle Demir took more coffee on board and continued.

"One of the soldiers was on his walkie-talkie almost constantly and he was giving the boss man details of exactly how much there was. There came a point when they all knew just how much they would be getting, and yes, they realised just what it would buy after the war."

Uncle Demir said every soldier would be able to buy a small farm with a house and the boss man would be rich beyond his wildest dreams.

We talked long into the night and watched as the sun came up over the Malë Ternovc mountain. It was then time to go home. As we stood in the doorway my uncle and my father embraced and my father started to weep.

"What is it brother?" Uncle Demir said. "We are alive and healthy, you should be happy not crying like a schoolgirl."

"But you have lost everything Demir, you have given it all away."

"And it was worth it," he said, "for I have saved the whole village and as you say they will write a book about me and I will be as famous as Mr Schindler in Schindler's List when they make my movie and who knows I might even play the starring role."

It was a much-needed injection of humour and we all laughed, even my father.

"I have my house and my farm and I still have my dear family and my health. I want for nothing more."

Father dried his tears and wrapped his arms around Nani and me as we walked out into the cold and started to make our way to the garden gate. As we were halfway down the garden path my uncle called out.

"Hey brother."

We turned around.

"You don't think I gave the silly bastards all of my gold do you?"

My father stuttered.

"Yes... I... I thought-"

Uncle Axhi was laughing.

"If you believe that my brother, then you are as stupid as those soldiers."

CHAPTER FOUR
DEATH OF A HERO

The rest of the day was a blur and although we talked a little about the events of the previous evening, most of the day was spent in silence with my father deep in thought, sitting at the kitchen table smoking and drinking copious amounts of Turkish tea. Several times he buried his head in his hands and let out a deep sigh and then looked at me with a forlorn look in his eyes. I couldn't remember ever seeing that look before.

"What is it Agi?" I asked on numerous occasions, but he'd refuse to answer me, shaking his head and returning his face to his hands.

In the end, I stopped asking.

Although I was physically exhausted, that evening sleep was hard to come by and when the sun peeked through the open curtains the following morning I felt as if I hadn't gone to bed. I almost crawled out from under the duvet and I so wanted to stay there but at the same time, I had an urge to get dressed and go out for a walk. I needed fresh air, I needed to walk through the grass and see the mountain again, I wanted to feel the wind and somehow realise that I was truly alive and not part of a dream.

My parents were sitting at the kitchen table and offered me some breakfast and tea but I refused. When I told them I was going out for a walk they looked worried but nevertheless didn't stand in my way.

"Be careful," my father said.

I wrapped up against the cold and ventured out. I wanted to walk up the mountain but somehow I couldn't bring myself to do it. Perhaps another time? Instead, I turned the other way and walked towards the centre of the village. I knew immediately that the atmosphere in the town of Veliki Trnovac had changed. To my surprise there were many people around, faces I recognised from the mountain the night before but there were also Serb soldiers everywhere. Their faces were uncovered so I knew I wasn't in any immediate danger but I wondered to myself if any of them had been there on the mountain the previous evening. I was conscious that I was staring at one or two of them and when they caught my eye I quickly averted my gaze.

I tried not to think about the incident on the mountain but it was difficult with so many army uniforms around. It also hit home that the very reason the Serb Soldiers had covered their faces meant that they were fully committed and prepared to carry out the despicable task they had been ordered to do. And forget the cause and the war and whatever false justification they were given, those beasts were ready and willing to shoot innocent men, women and children for money. Nothing else but money, my uncle's *deal* had proved that beyond doubt. I looked again at one or two of the soldiers and found myself loathing them.

As I walked down the main street I noticed one of my friends carrying a suitcase across the road.

I called out to her, to ask where she was going.

"Drita. Where are you going?"

"We are leaving Lurata, we have family in Macedonia and we will be safer there."

"What do you mean?" I said. "This is where you live, you can't leave."

She looked at me as if I was stupid.

"You were there when they were going to massacre us on the mountain?" She said sarcastically.

"Yes, but-"

"Then you know if it hadn't been for your uncle's money we would have all been murdered."

I had no answer for her as she continued.

"And you've heard what the Serb soldiers are doing to the Muslim girls."

"Yes…"

"It makes no difference to them, young or old. They are shooting husbands, fathers and brothers and raping the girls on the spot."

I took a sharp intake of breath. I'd never heard any of my school friends using that awful word, and because she had used it, it was as if it somehow brought it closer to home… more real. She lifted the heavy suitcase into the boot of a car that had pulled alongside. I recognised her parents and her young brother who was in Amir's class at school. Her mother gave me a little wave.

Drita spoke more quietly now.

"Sometimes they make the husbands and fathers watch as they take turns, it's as if it's all a bit of fun to them."

She pulled at her hair in an act of frustration and anger.

"The perverted psychopaths. Can you imagine what that must do to a father watching his daughter go through that?"

Drita climbed into the car and started to wind the window down as she leaned out and spoke again.

"I think I'd rather see my father killed before he had to endure that."

I was subconsciously nodding.

"Goodbye Lurata, and thank your uncle for us. We haven't had a chance to see him."

I stood frozen to the spot while the car disappeared from view and noticed that the road was unusually busy with cars packed to the roof, some with trailers and one or two even towing caravans crammed with their worldly goods. Some of the cars were bursting at the seams taking family members and friends without transport of their own. It seemed the whole of the town of Veliki Trnovac was on the move and it felt like the end of the world.

I took a lemonade in the local café and the talk was of nothing else but who was leaving town and who was staying. I was welcomed warmly as the niece of the man who had saved the entire population and they even refused payment for my drink. They told me the roads to Kosovo and Macedonia were crowded and then they told me to go home because the streets of Veliki Trnovac were no longer safe for a girl like me.

Back home I told my father everything I'd seen, everything I'd been told. He buried his head in his hands and sighed once more and then he looked up and spoke to me.

"You'll have to leave too."

At first, I thought he meant we were leaving as a family but then the truth dawned on me and I realised he meant just me.

"No way," I said. "No way am I leaving without you or Nani. If I'm going it's with you two, otherwise, I stay here."

My father was furious.

"How dare you question my authority, I'm your father just remember that and I know what's best for you."

My mother stood in the corner of the kitchen visibly shocked, but not visibly shocked at my father's words, visibly shocked that I had dared to answer him back in that way. I had never spoken to Agi like that, his word was always the last word and as always he knew what was best. And yet I still argued for all I was worth because the thought of leaving them behind was a pain I couldn't bear to imagine. I was in tears, as was Nani but my father would have none of it and said I was leaving the following morning. His face was red with rage.

"But why just me?" I said.

Agi paused for a few seconds.

"Because you're a girl that's why… you're more at risk than anyone else."

"But Nani's a girl why can't she go with me?"

My father cast a glance at his wife.

"She can go if she wishes, that's her choice, and she's old enough to decide for herself."

I looked at Nani who looked terrified and confused and yet I knew at that moment that she would never leave my father's side. I respected and admired her decision in a way but regretted that I was an only child. It would have been so much easier making the journey with a sibling or even two.

Late afternoon he brought a sports bag down from upstairs, a bag he had packed with food and clothes and of course money. The only thing that crossed my mind was that Agi never packed a suitcase… it was always Nani.

And the arguments started again because I knew now that this was for real.

"I won't go without you." I screamed with tears running down my face.

At this point, my father had been standing and I sensed he was about to say something important, perhaps one of those father-daughter lectures…but I was wrong. He returned to the table and slowly pulled out a chair. It seemed an enormous effort as he lowered himself into the seat and gazed across the room at me. A smile pulled across his face and then it was gone and he beckoned me to take a seat at the table with him. I walked over and sat down and he reached for my hands which he cupped in his. He spoke in a whisper. His words are still with me today as if they were spoken yesterday.

"My loçki, my beautiful perfect loçki. You know I love you with all my heart."

His eyes were full of tears, the anger having dissolved away in an instant. As he squeezed my hands tight the tears from his big brown eyes began to roll down his cheeks.

It was some time before he was able to get the words out but eventually he wiped his tears away, clenched his teeth and spoke.

"I'm not frightened of anything and I'll gladly accept death with both hands held high," he said. "They can't hurt me, no one can hurt me."

He leaned over the table took my face in his hands and kissed me on the forehead.

"But I can't bear the thought of watching you abused by them, I can't loçki."

We cried together and he took out a handkerchief and wiped my cheeks.

"I don't want to see that loçki, you understand?"

"Yes, Agi."

"Surely that's not too much for a father to ask of his daughter."

I shook my head. No words would form on my lips.

"So you will leave first thing tomorrow okay?"

Without wanting to I nodded my head just once.

"Good," he said. "that's settled. I will sleep all the better tonight."

We sat together at the kitchen table as a family and drank tea as if it were going out of fashion. I didn't even like tea but it was sort of expected, a bit like a final supper but without any supper because no one had the appetite for food. We sat holding hands, all three of us, parting occasionally to pick up a cup to take a drink. Eventually, I decided it was time to get ready for bed and prepared myself for the worst day of my life. No matter what my parents said to comfort me I still felt as if I was abandoning them, the people who meant more to me than the world itself.

My father's mobile phone rang just before midnight. It was late and my heart skipped a beat as I answered. It was Auntie Naxhia.

"Hi Auntie Naxhia, how are you?"

She asked for my father and I knew straight away something was wrong.

My father took the phone and within seconds he was at the door, pulling on his coat with one hand while holding the phone with the other.

"We'll be there right away," he said.

"What is it Agi?"

"Get your coat and the car keys Lurata, your Uncle Demir is ill. I'll get my medical bag."

Despite the winter conditions I jumped into the car dressed only in my pyjamas and no shoes and drove the short distance to my uncle's house. Auntie Naxhia was waiting for us, tears streaming down her face and she ushered us quickly to the second-floor bedroom where uncle's body lay at the side of the bed. My father was down on his knees straight away. Uncle Demir was conscious but not speaking and looked at us with a puzzled look on his face. He was grey and his body so cold to the touch and my auntie was shaking him by the arm.

"You're not leaving us Demir," she said over and over again.

"He's fine," my father kept saying. "You're going to be just fine Demir."

Father checked his vital organs and gave him a series of injections before telling us we had to get him into the car and over to the surgery. We carried him down the stairs and thankfully by the time we moved outside Uncle Demir was able to stand by himself and even managed to speak a few words.

"You're going to be fine Uncle Axhi." I said.

I drove as fast as I could to the surgery and nearly careered off the road at one point but we eventually made it and we helped him into the surgery. I remember Uncle Demir turned to me and grinned and said it was the first time he had ever been driven in a car by a woman.

In the surgery, father managed to get him to lie on a treatment table where he examined him some more and gave him another two injections. He appeared to have recovered well and was alert and communicating fine. I was so relieved.

"We still need to get him to a hospital." father announced. "Vranje is only thirty minutes away."

Father said he would drop me back home and he would go to the hospital with Naxhia. I objected, I wanted to go too but father said I had to go back and get Amir the next morning as he had been staying at a friend's house.

When I returned home I told Nani all the details but said that Uncle Axhi was fine. He'd perhaps need to stay in hospital for a few days but whatever had happened to him, he seemed to be over the worst.

Early the following morning my mobile phone rang. It was my father calling from the hospital. He had been there all night and as he spoke I knew there was something terribly wrong.

"You need to get Amir and bring him here now Lurata."

"What is it Agi, how is Uncle Axhi?"

"Just do as I say loçki."

I drove to the friend's house and knocked on the door. Poor Amir was in bed and she had to wake him. I explained about Uncle Demir and Amir got dressed and climbed into the car. Amir kept asking about his father and I didn't know what to say. I told him his father had been taken ill through the night and he was in the hospital at Vranje.

"How is Babi?" Amir kept asking. "Is he going to be okay?"

I kept telling him I didn't know but we'd find out soon. We pulled into the hospital and I drove into a parking bay, turned the engine off and quickly ran round to Amir who was struggling with his seatbelt. I helped him out of the car and he reached for my hand as we ran towards the hospital entrance.

About twenty-five yards from the hospital I looked up and saw my father and Auntie Naxhia standing by the doorway. I froze. My eyes fixed on Auntie Naxhia and I knew by the empty look in her tear-drenched eyes that my darling uncle was dead. I lost the power in my legs and fell to the ground. I couldn't breathe. It was as if a big hole had been bored into my stomach as if a part of me had died. Amir didn't know what to do, didn't know who to run to. I wanted to stand and be strong for Amir as he too collapsed in tears beside me.

"What is wrong?" he kept asking.

I looked into his beautiful deep brown eyes and wanted to tell him that everything was all right but it wasn't. Nothing would ever be the same again, not for me and not for Amir.

We buried Uncle Demir the next day in line with Muslim tradition. Everyone who had remained in Veliki Trnovac was there to pay their last respects. No one could quite believe that Demir had been taken so soon after what he had done. They were calling him a hero and one woman said that if anyone deserved to be taken into heaven then it would surely be him. She was saying that God was good and he would take special care of Demir.

I was confused and couldn't help thinking that God shouldn't have taken him at all.

My father's voice interrupted my thoughts.

"Lurata," he said gently, "we have buried your uncle."

"Yes, father."

"Now it's time to go."

CHAPTER FIVE
FORCED TO FLEE

My father had reluctantly allowed me one more night in the family home but it was of little comfort to me and I hardly slept at all. My mother came into my room just after seven in the morning and told me we were having a cooked breakfast as father had planned an early start for me.

She had cooked some eggs and buttered some toast but it would all remain un-eaten and instead, the eggs were sliced up and placed between two slices of fresh bread and pushed into my sports bag. I asked again if my mother was coming with me but she shook her head. I wondered if it would have been different if my uncle hadn't died. My father needed his wife with him, I knew that, but regardless, I don't think she would have left him whatever the circumstances. My father was giving me my final instructions.

"On no account must you use the main road until you get into Kosovo and you'll need to go over the top of the mountain."

"The mountain?" I asked incredulously.

"It's not far, thirty or forty minutes to the top and then you will be able to plan your route from there. You will see the main road from the top and you can chart a point or two and follow the road parallel until you are one hundred per cent sure you are in Kosovo and then and only then can you try and hitch a ride or take a bus to Pristina."

"But why can't I take a bus from the village?"

He was lifting my bag onto my back.

"Because your father knows best loçki."

I looked over at my mother who was standing by the door in floods of tears, tears that I thought would surely never dry. I was still asking questions, I was terrified at the thought of arriving in a city where I knew no one.

"Where will I go?"

"There are Red Cross centres," my father said. "Head for the centre of town and ask one of the NATO men or a policeman. There are camps for refugees in Pristina and you'll be safe there."

My father, the man who had always been my protector, was sending me off into the unknown and in an instance I knew that if he was prepared to do that then things in Veliki Trnovac must be pretty horrific.

I said an emotional goodbye to my mother. It lasted some time and I felt so warm and secure and safe as she wrapped her arms tight around me. She told me to buy a mobile phone as soon as I got to Pristina so that I would be able to call her. I wanted to stay there forever and felt sure that no harm could come to me as long as she held me in this way. I went to give my father a hug but he said he would walk with me for a while and we set off.

He kept repeating what he had told me about the Red Cross and how safe Pristina was. He also tried to justify his decision to stay, saying it was our home and it was all we had and if he left it, then the Serbs would loot the property and set it on fire. My parents had worked so hard on that property for so many years and as he told me the war would be over in a few months and everything would return to normal I almost believed him.

The path to the top of the mountain was clearly visible and about five hundred metres from the top Agi said goodbye. It was another emotionally charged moment as he held me as my Nani had done and we shed a flood of tears. As I reluctantly walked away from him I remember thinking I couldn't take much more and so wanted to turn around and run back.

I stood on the track for some minutes as I watched Agi disappear into the distance and then I dried my tears and slung my sports bag onto my back and started to walk. The path to the top looked a little daunting, very steep and not so well-trodden. I kept focussing, twenty, thirty, forty metres ahead and tried to pick out points. I was now more frightened of the wild animals than anything else. I had heard tales of wild dogs and an occasional wolf and every so often I would stop, try not to breathe and listen for sounds. Now the town of Veliki Trnovac didn't seem such a bad place to be.

I picked up my pace as the path zigzagged to the top and within about forty minutes I had made it to the crest of the mountain. It was cold, crisp and clear with four or five centimetres of snow under my feet but the view over into Kosovo was perfect and the sheer beauty of the scene took my breath away. The mountains were covered in a pristine, white blanket of snow and it contrasted beautifully with the deep green of the forests and the dead and dying deciduous trees and shrubs in various shades of red, yellow, black, orange, some even pink and magenta. I eased my bag from my shoulder, took out my waterproofs and spread it out on the ground and sat down. I stayed there for some time admiring the sheer beauty and enjoying the stillness and calm. Everything was so peaceful. Surely this place was too beautiful for a war?

I realised I was shivering and decided it was time to move on as I repacked my bag and took a final look at where I was heading. Agi had been right, the main road to Kosovo was clear enough to see but he had also emphasised how very dangerous it was and as I started walking downhill I made a mental note of the route. *Keep to the right of the road.* Agi had said. *Make sure you are well inside the Kosovo border before you break your cover.*

His words rang in my ears and I did as he had instructed but it was tough going. Once I reached the bottom of the hill the path petered out and I was walking through dense forest and bracken, taking my bearings from the noise of the traffic over to my left. I didn't want to get too close to the road but figured as long as I could hear traffic noise then I wouldn't stray too far. From the bottom of the mountain, Agi had said it was no more than four kilometres into Kosovo, but he said I should walk at least six or seven before making my way to the road. So I walked on for at least three hours, stopping now and again for a drink of water and even managing to build up a hunger and eat my breakfast sandwich. My bag felt really heavy at that point and

I laughed, as I looked at all the food my parents had packed. It was enough to feed a small army.

Despite the cold I was sweating hard and the path I had chosen appeared to gain a little altitude. I had an idea that it might be good to gain a little height as it might give me a chance to view the road again. It was tough going especially the long uphill climbs but I remembered my father telling me that every uphill has a downhill and I pressed on. On one steep, downhill stretch I missed my footing on a loose rock and pitched forward violently. I was aware of the ground rushing up towards my face but had the presence of mind to twist away from it and I landed on my back, my rucksack absorbing most of the impact. I lay for a second and realised I had gashed my ankle on a tree root. My father had had the presence of mind to pack me a small first aid kit and after patching myself up and drinking a little water I was on the move again.

I came to a clearing in the forest and noticed a path off to the left that appeared to climb even further. I followed it and sure enough, after about two hundred metres the forest opened up in front of me giving me a clear view of the main road no more than half a kilometre away. I caught my breath for a second. I couldn't quite believe the sheer volume of traffic heading into Kosovo. Cars, trucks and even motorbikes, bumper to bumper, slowly edging their way towards the border. The border checkpoint was obvious, a real build-up of almost stationary vehicles, the sound of tooting horns and the bright blue helmets of the NATO peacekeepers clearly visible. I confess I felt a little pleased with myself as I turned around and started walking again. Agi's instructions were good and I had followed them to the letter. I was in Kosovo now and I felt safe. I'd somehow get a ride to Pristina and everything would be all right.

I walked directly to the road and came out no more than two kilometres inside the Kosovo border. The traffic was very slow and almost immediately I noticed a bus crawling slowly towards me. He had no choice but to stop as I jumped in front of him. He opened the door with a smile on his face and spoke in perfect Albanian.

"You'll get yourself killed you silly girl."

I also spoke to him in Albanian.

"I'm sorry but I need to get to Pristina."

I fumbled in my bag for the money my father had packed and pulled out a 300 dinar note.

"I'm sorry I don't have any change."

The bus driver told me not to worry about money.

"We have NATO here now, we are free men so money is of no consequence to me at the minute."

He was grinning and told me to take a seat, he seemed so kind and he immediately put me at ease. He explained that he was heading for Gnjilane, which was thirty minutes away and from there I could take a bus direct to Pristina. I took a seat by the window and tried to blend in with the rest of the crowd on the bus.

As we neared Gnjilane, the traffic built up even more reducing the pace of the bus to no more than that of a snail. Every car, every truck appeared to be flying the Albanian flag from a window or an aerial and I couldn't quite understand that significance. We were in Kosovo, why not a Kosovan flag or why a flag at all?

As we pulled into Gnjilane the bus driver called me forward. He told me to be very careful and not to trust anyone. I remember being very frightened as I climbed from the bus and almost immediately I became aware that, although it was quite busy, there were very few women around and almost no girls of my age to be seen. Gnjilane was very rough, I didn't like the look of the men at all and the buildings appeared run down and neglected. Some of them were in ruins and bore the marks of bullet and mortar fire.

I started walking. It wasn't long before I spotted the NATO soldiers again which calmed my anxiety a little. They were American troops this time, bright blue helmets or baseball caps and tiny stars and stripes flags flying from the aerials of their trucks and the very sight of the explosion of colour in an otherwise dreary grey backdrop fascinated me. I had been a long-time admirer of anything American, particularly their movies that I had watched as a young girl. Rightly or wrongly I had always looked up to America, loved the way they spoke and adored their style, their colourful fashions and carefree attitude. Uncle Demir had always said he was going to take Amir and I to New York and it was something I had dreamt about for as long as I could remember. A jeep passed me with four young American soldiers on board. They were smiling and laughing and their teeth were shiny white and pretty... they were like movie stars.

Eventually, I found the bus to Pristina. There was a very long queue and once again I handed the bus driver my high-denomination dinar note. He wasn't as happy as the first bus driver, telling me off and saying I should have changed it at one of the local bars or shops. He was speaking Albanian too so I answered him in the same tongue and said that we were free now and that the United Nations were here and they had saved us and who cared about money anyway. It seemed to work as he reluctantly allowed me on board albeit with a grumble and a shrug of his shoulders.

After an hour we came across a huge military checkpoint. There were soldiers everywhere and the atmosphere on the bus could be cut with a knife as I heard someone say that we were pulling into a Serbian-populated town called Gracanica where there had been a lot of trouble. This time the traffic was heading in the other direction and it was convoys of Serbs fleeing for their lives as Kosovans and Albanians took out their frustration and bitterness on the town of Gracanica and the Serb men women and children who lived there. This was no different to what I was doing, fleeing from the town where I had grown up. It was utter madness, the futility of it all, how blind can man be?

I peered into the back of a large car as it passed by the bus window. There were five small children squeezed onto the back seat, the youngest about a year old and the oldest, a girl, probably no more than eleven years old. Like me, they looked lost, puzzled and were looking for answers to why their parents were running for their lives. My heart went out to the little ones.

It took over an hour to get through the checkpoint at Gracanica after two UN soldiers had meticulously checked the identification and documents of the bus driver. Twenty minutes after that, the bus driver announced that we were driving into the Pristina bus station.

I was aware that I was thirsty, so very thirsty, as I climbed from the bus. I had finished my last bottle of water just outside Gnjilane and that had been some hours ago. It was cold now too, and dark and I pulled my scarf tightly around my neck as I buttoned up my coat. I felt frightened and vulnerable as I looked around for somewhere to go. I didn't know what to expect but thought there might be some sort of information desk at the bus station or at least an employee to ask directions to the Red Cross people. There was nothing. I looked across the road and spotted a bar on the main pedestrianised street and thought at least I could get a drink of water in there. It was next to a large hotel and a police station. Someone would help me in there, I was sure of it.

As I opened the door I was hit by a wall of noise, not the peaceful tranquil scene I imagined as families took a quiet coffee on the way home for the evening. It was full of UN soldiers and policemen drinking beer that the bartender was pulling from a shiny silver pump perched on top of the counter. I had never seen anything like it before. The beer in Veliki Trnovac all came from glass bottles or tins and was only ever seen at a wedding or celebration. This was another world. I had never seen so much beer and it was obviously good because everyone looked as if they were having a wonderful time. It was as if the war outside had stopped at the doorway to the bar. I became aware that many people were staring at me as I walked in but nevertheless, the barman greeted me with a big smile. I asked for a water and he poured it from the tap saying there was no charge. He began talking to me and asking where I was from, and where I was going. I felt exposed and for some reason didn't have the confidence or courage to share my predicament with him. I looked at the UN soldiers and the policemen and for the first time since before the incident on the hill actually felt quite safe.

I emptied the glass of water and asked for another trying to pluck up the courage to walk over to a table of policemen and ask where the Red Cross Camps were. The barman was asking me more questions and clearly flirting with me. That was the last thing I needed, it was late and I needed to act fast if I was going to get shelter otherwise I'd end up sleeping in a bus station or worse, a shop doorway. In the end, I lost my nerve and wandered outside and propped myself up against the window feeling sorry for myself. Several minutes passed and I flopped to the floor. It was so cold on my backside but I didn't care. I would sit there until someone came to help me because I couldn't bring myself to walk back into the bar.

Ten minutes passed and two UN Police Officers came out and started speaking to me. They spoke in movie accents and although I couldn't understand a word they were saying, their voices were somehow soothing to me, especially the younger blond soldier who I felt an instant attraction too. Soon after a Pristina policeman joined them and he was also speaking English but he sounded so much more aggressive than the

Americans, a real contrast in the tones of their voices. One of the policemen returned to the café and came out with someone else who started talking in Albanian and he explained he was an official translator for the Americans. He asked me what I was doing and I said I wanted to know where the Red Cross Shelters were. The policeman spoke to me in Albanian and asked where I was from. When I told him he said that he couldn't help me because the Red Cross Camps were for displaced Kosovans and Albanians only and there was no way they could accommodate anyone from Serbia. I couldn't quite believe it as the policeman walked back into the café. I watched through the window as the barman poured him a beer and he returned to a table with his colleagues laughing and joking as if he didn't have a care in the world, as if he hadn't even met me.

Now it was the translator who sounded annoyed. He kept talking to the Americans and their voices grew louder and louder, their actions more animated.

He turned to me.

"You must go, these streets are dangerous."

I was puzzled.

"But I don't have anywhere to go," I said, "I don't understand, I am in Pristina and the Americans are here. Aren't we supposed to be safe?"

The translator frowned.

"If only it were that simple."

He was arguing with the Americans. I caught odd words. I'd picked up a little English from school and of course, the subtitled or dubbed movies. I heard the word *dangerous* many times and I began to get frightened. The translator was pointing at me and then to the far end of the street and the American soldiers were saying *No! No!* At one point the translator appeared to walk away but then quickly returned.

"You can't stay here all night," he said, "you'll have to leave."

It seemed a hopeless situation and I started to cry. The translator shook me by the shoulder.

"The Americans have said you can stay with them."

"What?" I said.

He repeated his statement.

"The Americans have a flat near here and they have said you can stay there tonight."

"No," I said, "that's not possible, it would not be right."

The translator let out a deep sigh and shook his head.

"Do you want shelter or not?"

"Yes."

"Then you haven't got a choice you stupid girl. There are no hotels open and the Red Cross don't want you."

He looked at his watch.

"I have to get going so tell me what you are planning to do."

He was right... I had no choice. It seemed like a crazy thing to do and yet as I stared at the two American soldiers long enough to be considered rude, I couldn't help but trust them. I nodded.

"Good," said the translator, "I might be able to go home to my family now."

The older of the soldiers reached for my bag and the other one turned to the translator who in turn spoke to me. "They said they will take care of you."

I nodded my head, dried my eyes and followed them across the street to their car.

CHAPTER SIX
GOD BLESS AMERICA

I sat in the back of the car, cold and nervous and yet I wasn't frightened. I somehow sensed that the two soldiers were the good guys and yet at the same time I couldn't help but mouth a silent prayer to The Almighty that my judgement would not let me down.

As soon as the car door closed paranoia set in. We were in the middle of a war and people were disappearing every day. It would not be beyond impossible for these two men to take me wherever they wanted, do whatever they wanted with me, kill me and create another statistic of a missing girl in a conflict that was spiralling out of control. I thought back to the mountainside on *that night*. On that particular night, my whole village very nearly became a statistic... a big one. It would be so easy for them and I tried my hardest not to burst into tears. As I pulled my coat tightly around my neck and snuggled into the thick collar, the seeds of doubt began to creep in and take root. My thoughts drifted back to my parents and I wondered how they were. Did they know something I didn't? Was that why they had sent me away?

I leaned against the cool window as the jeep pulled away and one by one the streetlights passed me by, blurred by the sheen of tears that filled my eyes. We were in the vehicle for no more than ten minutes during which I managed to convince myself that these men had freed Kosovo and driven the Serb Army back to the borders so they had to be the good guys. Just like in the movies and I had to trust them and the alternative, a doorway in a strange city seemed a whole lot worse and did not bear thinking about.

The car pulled into a gap on the side of the road and the older of the soldiers pointed to a six or seven-storey apartment that I assumed was where they lived. It wasn't what I expected. The street was narrow and very busy even at this time of night and would be described as poor Eastern European, certainly not the country environment I had been used to in Veliki Trnovac. I recall that we had to walk carefully through about two centimetres of mud. I looked around and the whole street was covered in mud which puzzled me. We were in the middle of a concrete jungle. Where had the mud come from?

A one-metre wide path led from the road to the entrance of the building that was dimly lit and a dirty pinkish colour. I looked at the Americans who gently herded me towards the door smiling and yet looking a little embarrassed at the dilapidated building where they lived. I somehow thought they might have been housed in some sort of plush barracks or a neat military complex, but no, it was an apartment on the ground floor in a depressed and tired street in a suburb of Pristina.

Ever the gentleman, the oldest of the Americans rushed forward to open the door to the block and as I took a final look up at the grotty building he took my bag and beckoned me forward. We walked through the door. Straight ahead were the stairs leading to the upper floors and to the left was a solitary door, which the blond soldier pointed to and took a step forward.

Although I had never set foot in a soldier's apartment it was probably how I would have imagined a place inhabited by two single men. It was a bloody mess! My God, my mother would have had a heart attack if she had seen where I would be spending my first night. We walked down a small narrow corridor and one of them stepped forward and opened the door to the lounge. I did my very best not to look too shocked and I thanked my lucky stars that it was dark as the look of amazement was clearly written all over my face. The sofa was piled high with dirty clothes, mainly camouflaged uniforms, but also undergarments, socks, t-shirts and several pairs of US army issue boots.

These two soldiers clearly liked a beer or two because the small coffee table was littered with empty cans. I looked into one of the corners and several unopened cases of beer sat alongside more dirty washing. They seemed not to notice as the man with the shaved head walked into the kitchen and returned with three cans of beer. He grinned a cheeky grin as he handed his colleague a can and offered one to me. I shook my head and he looked a little disappointed. As they drank their first can quite quickly they talked to each other and gave me an occasional glance. The two of them walked back into the kitchen and then quickly returned. They were pointing to the kitchen and making signs with their two hands cradled to their heads which I took to mean that this was to be my bedroom for the night. It made sense, I'm sure a kitten would have struggled to lie down on that sofa.

And so we sat down for the evening and we talked in two languages while I did my best to use the few English words I'd picked up at school and from the movies I'd seen. Surprisingly we got by. They had picked up a few Albanian words and we established each other's names quite quickly. They were called Brian and Peter and although they struggled at first with the pronunciation of Lurata, eventually they perfected it and after an hour I was conscious that I had smiled for the first time. Peter was the bald one with the cheeky smile, cheeky but nice and I warmed to him almost immediately. My judge of character had not let me down, now I was sure of it and as the seconds and the minutes and indeed hours ticked by I felt more and more comfortable in the grotty little apartment. Brian was altogether different, slightly younger than Peter and with more hair. He was quite handsome, a strong, confident man with deep blue eyes and I found myself staring at him more than I should have. I liked him immediately and by the end of the evening we were all good friends and I was completely at ease and knew I had made the right decision to stay the night with the two soldiers from America.

After a while, Brian and Peter indicated that we would be eating. I confess I had hardly eaten all day and my hunger had miraculously found itself again. Peter disappeared into the kitchen while Brian drank more beer and I sipped on my water. A little while later Brian reappeared with three plates of hot sliced, square meat and warm bread and butter. It was delicious and I managed to express the fact. They both started laughing and Brian produced an empty tin that read US Army Rations. It was cheap, mass-produced, processed meat meant for soldiers in the field but to me, it tasted like a meal from a five-star hotel.

Afterwards, we had US Army ration biscuits for dessert and then Brian made some coffee. To this day I will never forget my first dinner with the Americans, I can taste every morsel even now. Brian and Peter drank more beer after the coffee and Brian's eyes began to close as he drifted to sleep on the floor. Peter took control and brought me some blankets and pillows that he placed on the kitchen floor. He looked apologetic but I did my best to explain that it was fine and more than I could ever have hoped for just a few hours ago. He closed the kitchen door and I searched in my bag for my pyjamas. I washed and cleaned my teeth at the kitchen sink in between a mountain of dirty dishes, changed and slipped between the blankets as I lay my head on the pillow. I couldn't believe my luck. This was surely better than some freezing cold tent in the middle of a Red Cross Camp.

I slept well but woke in the early hours of the morning, stepping back in time and reliving the events of the day and the night before. At times I couldn't quite believe that I had agreed to accompany two strange men back to their apartment to spend the night and yet I knew I had no choice. At five in the morning,

I got up. I felt strangely invigorated and refreshed and set about the mountain of dishes as quietly as I could. There were so many it took me about thirty minutes. I packed my blankets and my pillow neatly into the corner, found some cleaning solution under the sink and set about an almost impossible task to put the kitchen back into working order.

It was around 8 am when Brian walked through with a look of surprise on his face. I'd made a good job if I say so myself and I shrugged my shoulders as if to say it was the least I could do. I was still working on a greased-up bench top as Brian tried to tell me to stop. I wasn't sure what he meant to say. Was he telling me I was wasting my time or simply telling me to take a break for some breakfast? There were eggs in the fridge and sliced bread so I cooked my friends some scrambled eggs and made toast and coffee. They sat at a kitchen table they had probably never seen for a long time and looked more than content. When they had finished, and with the aid of some paper and a pen they indicated that they needed to leave for work but said they would be back soon with the translator, the man we had seen the night before. Brian looked sad. I sensed I would probably have to leave with the translator and he knew it too. Perhaps he had found me alternative accommodation, a tent on a Red Cross Settlement or somewhere the police had arranged.

Before they left they sat me down under no circumstances was I to leave the building. It was a strange thing to say as I had no intention of leaving, I felt safe and secure and I had nowhere to go but they were adamant and

I remember thinking how serious they both looked. Did they know something I didn't?

And then they were gone. It was quiet and I felt lonely again so I did the only thing I could think of to take my mind off my imminent departure into uncertainty - I cleaned the apartment from top to bottom. I washed dirty uniforms and pressed clean ones and I polished boots and tables and ornaments and I vacuumed the entire place with a frenzy that almost burnt out the motor. I washed rugs and hung them out to dry on the balcony and I even cleaned the toilets.

Just after eleven in the morning, they arrived back with the translator, I found out he was called Visar. He looked even more miserable than he had the night before and as I suspected, he told me I couldn't stay with the Americans for another night. While he talked to me I noticed that Brian and Peter were walking around the apartment shaking their heads. They were laughing. Brian picked up his clean-pressed uniform and was showing it to Peter, grinning.

"It is time to leave now Lurata," Visor said.

"Where am I going?"

The translator was more than a little evasive and clearly unsure where they were going to put me. I felt strangely at home in my small apartment in a side street in the middle of Pristina even though I had been there less than twelve hours. It was clean and tidy and there was food in the fridge and I almost smiled as I told myself I even had my own two personal bodyguards.

"So where am I going?"

Visor shrugged his shoulders.

"We will take you to the police station and -"

Brian interrupted, I caught a few words and he was clearly questioning him.

"No," Visor said, "that is out of the question, it would be improper."

"What is it?" I asked.

Visor sighed.

"He said you should stay here but I won't allow it. It's not right. You're a young girl and they are grown men and if this got out there would be a scandal."

They were arguing even harder and the two Americans had raised their voices and were clearly intimidating the translator who was flinging his arms around in frustrated animation.

He turned to me.

"I won't allow it. The Americans can't just decide to grant board and lodgings to any girl they like the look of."

It was clear what he was insinuating but he couldn't have been further from the truth. These men were not like that. Even after such a short time in their company, I trusted them with my life. At one point the Americans even stood between us as if preventing him from getting to me.

Eventually, Visor turned to me.

"I can't stop you from staying here but I warn you, you are making a serious error of judgement."

I looked at Brian and Peter.

"I'll stay."

Visor translated my words to Brian and Peter and they broke out into broad beaming smiles as they hugged me spontaneously. Soon after Visor left and I made Brian and Peter some lunch with the groceries they had brought in. We sat around the table grunting out single-syllable English words and an odd Albanian phrase and I laughed inwardly at the crazy situation I had found myself in.

During the next few weeks my English improved considerably, learning basic words such as good, help, okay, thank you, son, daughter, friends and one word that cropped up rather too often – *dangerous*. I made a real effort to study the language and when Brian and Peter were out on duty after I had cleaned and tidied, I made a point of tuning into the English-speaking television and radio stations and practised stringing sentences together. I also helped Brian and Peter extend their basic Albanian vocabulary and within a month we were holding decent conversations.

During that first month, I didn't venture out of the house. This was because of strict instructions from Brian and Peter. They said it was a lawless Pristina I had ventured into, despite the UN peacekeeping troops and they told me in no uncertain terms that I was to go out without them. This was quite frustrating because I still hadn't been able to buy a mobile phone. I would text my mother from Brian's cell phone and had a couple of messages back from her but it was a UN issue phone and for some reason, the reception wasn't good enough to hold a conversation.

I can recall the day with clarity when they took me to a US Army base. It was a bright, sunny day and both Brian and Peter had a day off. We enjoyed an enormous dinner and on the way back we called into a shop where I purchased a cheap mobile phone and a pay-as-you-go   SIM card with twenty dollars credit on it. I remember sensing how nervous Brian and Peter seemed as they stood guard, almost like sentries outside the shop, while I waited to be served. I thought nothing of it at the time but those memories would come back and disturb my sleep for many years. If only I had sensed how dangerous the streets of Pristina really were.

It was the longest I had ever gone without hearing my dear mother's words and I broke into tears at the sound of her soft, calming voice. She cried too. She passed me to my father and between the tears I managed to tell him everything was fine and that I was safe and being well looked after. I told him how lucky I had been in finding my American saviours and he was relieved to hear that I wasn't in the middle of a field in a tent in the harsh camps of a Kosovan winter. I asked the question I had longed to ask for many weeks – *can I come home?* Nani simply said soon. She explained that the situation was improving and that the borders were now open but things weren't quite back to normal.

"We will come to see you soon," she said. "You must text the address and we will get there somehow."

I shed more tears as I said my goodbyes all too soon. It was strange, it was as if I had run out of conversation despite not speaking to them for so long but I hung on Nani's final words that we would meet up soon.

During the coming weeks, the tension appeared to ease a little and I ventured out with Brain and Peter quite a lot, but always in the car. We returned to the Army base several times and even went to dinner with some of their friends. As each new excursion passed without incident I convinced myself I'd be returning home soon and everything would be as I remembered as a small girl. There would be no war and no Serb soldiers and Veliki Trnovac would still be the beautiful place near the mountains that I loved so much.

Two weeks after that first phone call with my parents my phone rang very early one morning and my mother announced that she and my father were on a bus that had left Veliki Trnovac two hours earlier heading for Pristina. I was so excited and couldn't wait to tell Brian and Peter. Nani had said the journey would only take an hour more at the most and I begged Brian and Peter to somehow get the day off work so we could all eat together. I was so grateful, and yes, proud of my American friends and I so wanted my parents to meet them. I owed them so much, they couldn't begin to understand how much I loved them, they were like brothers to me. They telephoned their base and somehow managed to convince their commanding officer that they couldn't make it in that day. There was a slight problem in that I couldn't explain to my parents where it was we actually lived but Peter telephoned Visor who in turn called my mother and guided her to a road where we could all meet up safely. It was such an emotional meeting as we hugged and cried together. Eventually, we managed to prise ourselves apart and I introduced the two American soldiers to my beautiful parents. We climbed in the UN Jeep and drove the short distance to our apartment in Pristina.

Nani had cooked her favourite dish, *Sarma*, a cabbage marinated in mincemeat and spices and wasted no time in making herself at home in the kitchen. She put the huge dish in the oven and turned it up high that crisped the top of the cabbage and mince perfectly, and she served it as Brian and Peter brought out some wine and of course a few beers. I acted as a very poor, but I suppose adequate translator. It was an altogether perfect day, the war could have been a million kilometres away and my father constantly thanked Brian and Peter for looking after me, almost to the point of embarrassment. As we were almost finished I handed Agi a photograph of the soldiers and said he could keep it. Agi looked at it for a few seconds and then cried as he slipped it into his jacket pocket.

There were more tears at the dinner table that day when Nani announced that my cousin, Don, had been shot and killed at an army checkpoint. I had been very close to him, almost like brother and sister and I cried for some time while Brian and Peter tried to console me. Agi said he had been killed in his car - shot dead at close distance by automatic gunfire and he also said that many people had simply disappeared.

Don, was a businessman and it all seemed so senseless, he wasn't a threat to anyone. Agi said the soldiers who had killed him wore white sneakers… training shoes. I frowned.

"What is that supposed to mean?" I said.

Agi shrugged his shoulders. Brian nodded as if he knew exactly what Agi was inferring.

"What?" I asked.

Brian said that it wasn't just politicians and soldiers who had orchestrated and kept the conflicts running. Serbia and Kosovo and the rest of the autonomous regions were being overrun by lawless gangs hell-bent on making money from the many wars that had broken out, claiming they were behind a cause.

"It has been the same since the word war was first coined," Peter said. "During the second world war, most Nazis were more interested in growing rich than anything Hitler, Goebbels or Himmler proposed. There were more gold and art treasures stolen, stored or filtered through places like the Vatican and Switzerland than at any stage in history."

Agi was nodding his head as I translated exactly what Peter was saying.

"He's right," Agi said, "it's been said that it's the rich that wage war while the poor die."

I translated again.

Brian nodded.

"So true. Every war in history is undertaken for the acquisition of wealth. There are no exceptions."

I sat back in my seat exasperated and it hit me hard. This was why my father had sent me away, this was why Uncle Demir had given over his life savings and this was why Brian and Peter had almost kept me prisoner for the last two months. They feared for my safety. The men who had taken us to the mountain and had been ready to kill us were in it for the money, nothing more. The soldiers in the white sneakers… it somehow started to become clear.

As I helped Nani clear the dishes and she produced a bag of sweet pastries I asked her when it would be safe to come home.

"Listen to your father," she said. "Listen to your American friends. You can come home when it is safe to do so and not before."

Brian was standing in the doorway. It was almost as if he had understood every word my mother had just said.

"And promise me you'll never leave this place without me."

I looked up and smiled as a pleasant shiver ran the length of my spine.

"I promise. I promise."

CHAPTER SEVEN
TAKEN

I was in the bathroom getting showered and then dried when I overheard a conversation between Brian and Peter. They never normally talked about the politics inside the four walls of the apartment and in general I never asked. It was almost as if they had pulled down an invisible shield to protect me from the evils just outside the front door. But this morning I opened the door slightly and listened.

Brian was saying that by now the K.L.A. were thousands strong. They had detention camps in Albania in the towns of Durres, Vlore and Kukes. He said he'd heard stories that some of these detention centres were more sinister than they looked from the outside. The Kukes detention facility was a key supply point for the KLA during the conflict and the UN had been asked to investigate rumours that as many as fifty people had been tortured and murdered while they were detained by the KLA in Durres.

Peter mentioned one of the commanders; a man by the name of Azem Kupi who it was said mistreated and tortured prisoners there. He said he had more information from an escapee that Kupi had also abducted Kosovan Serbs in northern

Albania and sent them to a concentration camp called Daphne in Drenica, where he allegedly participated in the executions and torture of the non-Albanian population, removing their organs and selling them on the black market.

I took a sharp intake of breath. I remembered *'Arsal the Exaggerator'* had mentioned something about people's organs being removed too. I laughed to myself. Surely Arsal's tall tales could not have reached this far?

Brian had been busy in the kitchen by the time I had dressed. He was standing over by the cooker and served some eggs and beans onto three plates. He'd made a pot of coffee and made me sit at the table while he served me my breakfast.

I had had a soft spot for Brian from the moment I set eyes on him and living in such close proximity to him for many weeks it was inevitable that my feelings would develop even further. Brian was a single man and during the whole time I stayed in the apartment there was not one single mention of a girlfriend back home in the States or indeed a girl here in Pristina. Neither Peter nor Brian ever brought any girls around

to the apartment and I knew that to be strange in itself as there was plenty of talk about the local prostitutes and their American colleagues in the military camp and what they got up to in their spare time.

The chemistry that developed between us was truly magical and whereas Peter was undoubtedly my hero, our relationship was always like brother and sister or even father and daughter like. I was very tearful in those first few weeks, having never been away from my home or my family before and Peter would reach out for me and hold me for hours, wiping away the tears that ran down my face. I felt so comfortable in Peter's arms but there was never any question of it going any further. With Brian it was different and I purposely avoided any intimacy with him as I suspected where that might lead. Nevertheless, there were lots of occasions where we would be thrown close to each other, like sitting together on the sofa watching TV or within touching distance of each other in the tiny kitchen, washing a few dishes or tidying up and as the weeks turned into months the sparks undoubtedly began to ignite. At times it was almost as if a surge of electricity passed between us.

One day I had a crazy idea to try one of their uniforms on. As you can imagine they were too big for me but it all seemed a great laugh at the time. Both Peter and Brian were in their respective bedrooms, working on their computers and I had the notion to march into their rooms saluting, giving them a little laugh. They'd had a particularly long, hard day and I wanted to cheer them up. I had almost finished when I noticed Brian standing in the doorway and I was most embarrassed. I had been caught before I'd been able to perform my act.

"I'm so sorry," I said, "I'll take it off."

"*Jo jo jo une te ndihmoj.*" he said which means "no no no I'll help you."

He walked over and reached for the belt around my waist and as he tightened it and rearranged the jacket I couldn't stop looking at his face. The smell of his aftershave mixed with his natural body odour was intoxicating to me and it was almost as if someone had flicked a switch inside me. I couldn't take my eyes off him.

"What's wrong?"

He noticed me staring.

"I don't know," I said, "I've never felt this way about a man before."

As soon as the words tumbled out of my mouth I wanted to take them back but I couldn't and the way I looked at him left him under no illusion that I had felt an enormous attraction to him. It was an awkward moment. He raised his blue magnetic eyes and smiled his beautiful perfect smile and said *Shume mir,* which means very good. It didn't even make sense. He placed his fingertip on my lips as if telling me not to say anything else. By that point, I was emotional and feeling weak at the knees and it took all my willpower and strength to turn around and walk away. I was falling hopelessly in love with Brian as much as I wanted to fight it. He reminded me of my first love back in Veliki Trnovac, a beautiful boy called Orki. These were the same feelings I had experienced back then… even at nine years of age!

"I'll show Peter."

That was all I could think to say as I walked in the direction of his room, my heart pounding out of my chest.

As soon as Peter saw the oversize uniform hanging from my skinny frame he thought it was a great laugh and started taking pictures as I saluted him. He placed the blue beret on my head and even painted a little moustache on me as he tried to teach me the military way of standing at ease, and then to attention. That awkward moment with Brian had passed and I breathed a sigh of relief.

After a little time, I went to take off the uniform. Brian stepped forward to help with the fiddly belt as Peter wandered back to his bedroom. I remember leaning against Brian while he unbuckled the belt in the hope he would hug me and as if by magic he did and I melted into his arms as he held me so tight, sighing quietly. After a few minutes we parted and as he looked into my eyes he put his hands on my face and kissed both cheeks allowing his lips to linger and drift across my skin. I was so lost in that tender moment and desperately wanted to kiss him. So I returned his kisses on his cheek, but dangerously close to his lips in the hope I would get a positive response. Brian closed his eyes and searched for my lips with his. He kissed me so tenderly, his lips so soft and I was frozen in heaven as our kissing became more passionate and he hugged me tighter and tighter as we fought for breath. I wanted the moment to last forever especially as his lips moved to my neck but then as quickly as it had started he stopped, taking my hands in his and kissing both of them in turn. Then he simply walked away.

It was inevitable that we would kiss again and we did at every given opportunity when we found ourselves alone. On one occasion we managed to sleep together in his room though we both made a vow that nothing sexual could or would happen. I lay next to Brian and we caressed each other and then fell asleep as he held me in his arms all night.

A few days later Peter and Brian sat me down and said I would have to go. I was in shock and more than confused. I wanted to tell Brian that I never wanted to leave him but of course, I couldn't because Peter was there and I assumed he knew nothing of our intimate embrace. Peter appeared very rational and explained that the UN had found out about our arrangement which was very much against the rules. Brian sat on the corner of the sofa quietly nodding but said nothing.

The atmosphere over the coming days was very strained and I longed for Brian to take me in his arms and tell me he'd worked something out so that we could be together but he never did. I couldn't understand it, Brian was a single man and although there was a bit of an age gap we were very much alike in personality and our outlook on life. I put two and two together and assumed he didn't have the same feelings for me as I had for him.

To make matters worse, when I phoned Nani and asked her if I could come home she said categorically no. Things still hadn't returned to normal and under no circumstances was I to attempt a return. I cried myself to sleep in the kitchen that night and woke up early the next morning with a headache from hell. Two days prior, in Brian's arms I had been the happiest girl in the world and now I felt I was about to lose him forever. There were dozens of questions flying around my head, not least, where would I stay, when could I return home but the worst question banging around my head like a big bass drum was would I ever see Brian again?   The thought terrified me.

I cooked Brian and Peter scrambled eggs for breakfast then I drank coffee but ate nothing. The thought of food made me feel sick. We had breakfast in silence but a couple of times I asked Brian and Peter where I would go. They didn't know, they said they would contact the translator and he would sort something out. I looked out of the window and the rain and sleet hammered against the glass windowpane which depressed me even further. It was still winter, albeit towards the end of the season and I knew that conditions in the UN refugee camps, in those canvass tents, were hell on earth. No heating, damp and miserable with a cold water shower block and one or two toilets for a hundred people or more. As my mind played tricks with me and I thought of the very worst scenario I burst into tears.

Peter tried to comfort me.

"Hey Lurata, don't be silly we won't throw you out into the street. We'll make sure you are safe and if you don't like where they put you, you can always come back."

I looked at Brian expecting a nod or a smile, but he sat there in silence. I noticed his omelette hadn't been touched. I wanted to reach out and touch him, I wanted to say 'te dua shume,' *I love you* and I felt my heart breaking apart.

Soon after they changed into their uniforms and got ready to leave. Just before they did there was yet another power cut and I lit a few candles. It was becoming an almost daily occurrence and although it was daylight it was still a dark gloomy morning.

As Brian walked towards the front door he turned to face me.

"Don't be going outside," he said. "Wait until we get back, we'll work something out."

I moved towards him and gave him a hug. He didn't respond at all. I wanted him to smile, I wanted him to take me in his arms and hold me, I wanted him to kiss me. Instead, he pushed me away and reached for his blue beret on a hook by the door and disappeared into the gloom of the corridor. How could he have been so cold? As the door closed I burst into tears again.

By midday, the electricity still wasn't on. I couldn't wash, I couldn't vacuum, I couldn't even watch any television or turn the radio on. Eventually, I decided I had to get out of there. I was bored rigid and sad and depressed and confused and craved some fresh air and a change of scenery. There was a newspaper kiosk less than five metres from the building. I'd buy a magazine. What was the worst that could happen in five metres? I'd buy a magazine and be upstairs back in the apartment within a few minutes.

I took my coat from the stand by the doorway and opened the door. I was nervous. For three months I had not left the apartment unaccompanied and as I walked down the stairs I noticed that I was breathing quite heavily. I told myself not to be so stupid. This was a UN safe area, I was buying a newspaper from a kiosk less than ten seconds from our front entrance, not making my way to the other side of the city.

"Don't be so silly," I mumbled to myself as I walked through the interior doors and walked towards the door that led to the main street.

The street was quite busy which put me at ease a little, people were going about their normal business and I noticed the small newspaper kiosk almost immediately as I buttoned up my coat against the biting wind and took a step forward. I fumbled for the loose change in my pocket and skirted a parked car which for some reason had stopped on the pavement. I thought it unusual and yet we were living in the middle of a troubled city and parking fines were the last things on anyone's mind.

The kiosk was quiet, the vendor and just one other person. A black van drove towards the kiosk and stopped on the pavement to the left side of me blocking my way. This was ridiculous I thought. Why is everyone parking on the pavement? I looked down the street. There were plenty of parking spaces; the driver didn't need to stop there. Suddenly the van lurched forward and came careering towards me and I jumped back as I thought it was about to hit me.

"What the -"

In an instant, it screeched to a halt and the side door was flung open violently as two men leapt onto the pavement and ran towards me. One of them was holding something, something black and as he grabbed me he forced a hood over my head. I screamed for help as time seemed to stand still. I could hear the noise of the traffic and the hustle and bustle of a normal city street and I heard a scream that quickly died away and I heard one of the men swearing at me in Albanian with a Kosovan dialect. What was going on? Surely they had made a mistake? Suddenly I was off my feet and had no control of where I was going. I was up in the air... flying, and I winced as my upper body connected with the hard floor of the bottom of the van, sheer terror coursed through my veins as I heard the door slam shut and the driver laughed as he pushed the vehicle into gear and sped away.

"We've got her. We've got the fucking bitch."

They were laughing, the driver, the two kidnappers and another voice from the rear of the van. I felt a blow to the side of my head.

"Fucking spy whore."

I was trembling, shivering with fear trying to get my breath and longing for words that would not form in my mouth. It was as if I had turned into a mute. I wanted to beg for my life, protest my innocence, telling these men they had made a mistake and they had the wrong person but my mouth was as dry as a bone and my tongue stuck to the roof of my mouth.

The kidnappers were congratulating themselves on a job well done and hurling abuse at me from all directions, even the driver joined in the tirade of verbal cruelty.

I lay still and silent as the van picked up speed and I remembered Brian's warning over the many weeks. He knew something I didn't and had warned me time and time again. How could I have been so stupid?

Although the journey seemed to take a lifetime it couldn't have been more than ten minutes before the van skidded to a halt. I still hadn't managed to utter a single word and lay in the back of the van whimpering and sniffling. I heard my kidnappers open the door and they jumped out. Two hands reached in and dragged me across the metal floor by the hair.

"Come with me you fucking whore and don't give me any trouble or I'll cut your pretty face to fucking ribbons."

I'd never met these men. I'd never wronged them or upset them in any way. I remember being frightened and yet sincerely believing there had been an awful case of mistaken identity and soon everything would be rectified and I'd be taken back to Brian and Peter very quickly. I just needed to stay calm and wait for an opportunity where I could point out the mistake.

I still had the hood on as they pulled me through the opening of the van, my head banging on something as I yelled out in pain.

"Shut the fuck up."

I was dragged across some rough stony ground, they didn't give me a chance to stand and one of my shoes came off and I felt the sharp stones dig into my toes. I cried out for them to slow down, and told them I would walk but they took no notice as they almost ran to wherever it was they were taking me. We went through a series of doors and I remember being dragged along a corridor. Another door then opened and I was thrown into a room where I lay petrified in silence for several minutes. I whimpered like a badly scolded puppy, not daring to move and wondered how long it would be before they discovered the error of their ways.

I became aware of another door opening and footsteps and then a different voice and another period of silence.

"Take her hood off," someone said in Albanian.

I was sitting on the concrete beside a large dark red rug. I remember thinking it was like the colour of an apple gone bad. My knees were cold and stinging and I edged forward so that they rested on the edge of the rug. I could smell acrid cigarette smoke and foul body odour.

"Good," someone said, "make yourself comfortable."

I looked up slowly. There were two men in front of me standing at either side of a table. They were tall and skinny and I noticed that none of them wore uniform, which unnerved me a little. I don't know why, especially after the night on the mountain with Uncle Demir when everyone wore a uniform but somehow I wanted to see a uniform, a soldier, a policeman, it didn't matter. But I didn't see any. There was another man standing in the corner leaning on a wooden chair. He wore a leather jacket and jeans with elegant, well-polished black shoes. I took a sharp intake of breath as a trickle of perspiration ran down the back of my neck.

Another man sat at the table fiddling with a pen. He was by far the most menacing of anyone in the room and the others stayed silent while he stood and slowly walked towards me. I will never forget his face, it will come with me on my deathbed, I just know it and before he even spoke I knew he was one of the most evil creatures on God's planet.

He limped towards me, his dark greasy hair lay lank over one side of his face and his day-old stubble gave him a filthy look as he approached me smiling, looking at me from the corner of his eye.

He grinned as he spoke slowly in barely a whisper.

"We know what you've been doing."

He bent over me.

"Are you a whore?"

I shook my head.

"A fucking Serbian bitch whore?"

"No... I...I..."

I tried to form a constructive sentence but the words wouldn't come. The man's words resonated evil in every syllable, he terrified me from the outset and it was as if my throat closed before I could produce a single word.

"You've been fucking those Americans, haven't you?"

"No… please."

We've been watching you, you fucking Serb bitch."

At last, I found my tongue and managed to blurt out a few words.

"I'm not Serbian, I was born in Macedonia, I speak Albanian like you, my mother teaches the Albanian language and I -"

I didn't get another word out as the man stepped forward and punched me hard in the face. I had never been punched before in my life. It was like a bomb going off in my head as the blow physically lifted me from my knees, as I catapulted backwards smashing my head against a chair. I lay in a daze. The pain didn't register, just the shock and the numbness of it all. I started crying again as the men goaded my attacker who they called Azem to attack me again.

And he did. Azem lifted me up by the hair and punched me several times around the head as I cried out for mercy and tried to tell him there had been a terrible mistake. He beat me and kicked me for several minutes until he was out of breath and small droplets of sweat dripped from the end of his nose. I begged him to tell me what he wanted. I pleaded with him to ask me anything, anything at all and I would tell him the truth and surely my answers would convince him that I wasn't a Serbian spy.

Azem returned to the table as I lifted myself back onto my knees crying and begging him for mercy. I looked down and noticed that my clothes were stained with blood and a small crimson pool had begun to congeal in the centre of the rug. My lips were swollen and my cheeks were stinging where he had slapped me. Azem showed me no mercy. He allowed me to beg and whimper like a dog for five minutes while he sat in silence and then resumed where he had left off. My interrogation and the hands of Azem Kupi (I found out his full name later) lasted for more than an hour and it was a pattern of abuse he had clearly used before. He beat and kicked and punched and slapped and stamped on me for two to three minutes and then he would stop. He'd talk softly to me and ask me questions about the Americans and my activities as a spy. I'd relax and assume he'd take notice of what I was saying and I'd tell him anything he asked about the Americans, I said they were my friends and they'd rescued me when I came to Pristina and gave me a roof over my head and looked after me. I told him the truth. I told him I was not a spy but a simple village girl from Veliki Trnovac.

"Veliki Trnovac," he said.

"Yes."

"In Serbia?"

"Yes."

Azem nodded.

"Serbian bitch. A Serbian fucking spy."

"No, I, I was born in -"

Before I could say another word he was in my face shouting and screaming abuse and calling me the vilest names anyone could imagine. For the next fifteen minutes or so there was no physical violence just a prolonged assault of verbal mistreatment during which I sobbed and begged him to believe me. In many ways, it was worse than the beatings, which of course came soon after. There was a short respite and then he'd start with the gentle questions again, the same questions he'd already asked over and over again and I'd give exactly the same answers convincing myself if I told him enough times then surely he'd eventually believe me.

Azem Kupi wasn't a fit man and towards the end of that first hour, the interrogation and his efforts when he had beat me had clearly taken their toll. He was breathing hard and sweating profusely as he sat leaning against the table. And yet he was still smiling. He looked around at his men who somehow seemed to sense what was coming next. The man in the leather jacket stared at me with a strange look on his face.

Azem looked at him and grinned.

"Okay," he said, "rape the whore."

"No," I screamed, "no please -"

"Rape the fucking whore."

The men were on me like a pack of wild dogs. This was clearly something they had been waiting for and I wondered how many other poor girls had suffered at their hands. They ripped my jacket off and pinned me to the floor as I tried to kick them away. It was a hopeless cause as one of them sat on my stomach squeezing my breasts as another unbuckled the belt to my jeans. Kupi was shouting instructions of encouragement.

"Take your time boys, I want this spectacle to last a while."

I tried to scream out but one of the men had his fingers in my mouth.

I could see Kupi laughing.

"See how she likes the Kosovan cock as opposed to a Yankee one. Make sure she's fucked good and hard."

I remember a moment of sadness as I realised these were more or less my fellow countrymen, the history of Kosovo was intertwined with that of its neighbouring regions. Kosovo and Albania had been brothers for centuries and my tormenters spoke the same language as I did and by the sound of their names, worshipped the same god as me. There was no doubt these men were Albanian-speaking Muslims and they were treating me like an animal, a piece of meat. I recalled my Uncle Demir telling me once to "beware of your own dog", because "he is the one more likely to bite you". One of them ripped at the buttons on my shirt exposing my breasts. Their inhuman treatment was in marked contrast to that of the Americans, a country on the other side of the world, the foreigners, as they were known. They had shown me nothing but respect, love and kindness.

Kupi was in his element screaming and laughing as they ripped my jeans off and I could feel their hands groping at my breasts and their cold slimy fingers sliding into my panties.

The man with his fingers still in my mouth had inched closer to my face and I could smell the stench of his foul breath as he spoke.

"You fucking Serb whore, I'm going to fuck you like you've never been fucked before."

I don't know what came over me but I bit down hard with all my might. As the pain registered he screamed out, ripping his bloody fingers from my mouth and I managed to scream out.

"I'm no fucking whore I tell you, I'm a virgin."

I don't know what happened but suddenly the assault seemed to stall. Even Kupi looked shocked.

"What did you say?"

"I can't be a whore," I repeated, "I'm a virgin."

Kupi stood.

"Well, well. A little virgin."

"I'm not a whore, I've been trying to tell you that for the last hour."

Kupi walked over.

"Repeat that again."

"I'm nobody's whore."

He knelt down.

"Yes, you are."

"No I'm not."

Kupi edged closer. His teeth were stained yellow and brown and his body odour mingled with the smell of blood and his breath and the sweat of the other men and I did all I could to prevent myself from vomiting there and then.

"You are somebody's whore," he said leering at me, "now you're Azem's little whore."

* * *

The fact I'd disclosed I was a virgin seemed to change everything. The attitude of the other men and Azem Kupi had changed. Perhaps now they believed me I thought. They clearly didn't like the Americans for some reason but now they knew I hadn't been sleeping with them and had perhaps mellowed them. Kupi ordered his men to leave me and they threw me the clothes they had torn from me. I breathed a huge sigh of relief and dressed quickly.

Within ten minutes we were on the move and Kupi took me by the arm as he led me out of the building. He was carrying the black hood but at no point did he attempt to put it on me. As he led me towards a large jeep I looked back to see where they had been holding me. It looked like an old military establishment, run-down, dirty and in need of a lick of paint. It stood on its own grounds and as I looked to my left I could see the city of Pristina about half a kilometre away and a little closer, what looked like a hospital and a school. Despite the ordeal I'd gone through I began to feel a little more relaxed. Since my disclosure about being a virgin, there had been no more abuse, physical, mental or indeed sexual.

As we walked towards the car Kupi spoke to me normally. He didn't shout or scream nor did he insult me.

"Get in the car. Everything will be fine."

I sat in the back with two of his men on either side of me and Kupi sat in the front with the driver as we moved off. We drove in the direction of Pristina which reassured me even more. I convinced myself these men were plain-clothes policemen and now they had established I was just another refugee seeking shelter they would take me to a police station and telephone Brian and Peter to come and get me and it would all be over. I asked Kupi where we were going. He stared at me hard but said nothing and I thought it best to keep quiet as the buildings of Pristina loomed up in front of us.

We pulled up outside what looked like another rundown apartment block.

"What's this?" I questioned. "This isn't a Police Station."

One of the men laughed.

"No, and we certainly aren't policemen."

Kupi told him to shut up. He looked at me.

"Didn't I tell you everything would be fine?"

Because they still hadn't put a hood back on me I still wasn't too concerned. We all walked towards the building. Kupi walked in front and the other men flanked me. I thought about running but I knew I had no chance. They took me up about four flights of stairs, as it was clear the lift wasn't working with several wires hanging out of the push button control panel. It was a horrible place. I thought Brian and Peter's apartment block was a bit run down but this was on a different scale and the stairs smelled of stale urine. I recoiled in horror as we stopped in front of a large steel door with a barred iron grill.

"No please," I said, "you can't put me in there, I'm claustrophobic and-"

"Relax," Kupi said, "it's not a cell it's an apartment. That door is for security purposes."

He produced a bunch of keys and threw them to one of his men who proceeded to unlock the heavy door. It opened towards the outside and swung to the left. He pushed it flush with the outside wall and then removed the bunch of keys searching for another. Within half a metre of the steel door was another one, a wooden one, more in keeping with a standard apartment door. This door pushed in over and the man opened it and walked in.

"Where are we?" I asked. "Why are you taking me in there?"

Kupi smiled and pushed me in.

"This is my apartment, didn't I tell you everything would be fine. Now you are Azem's little whore."

Any thought of rescue or being taken to a Police Station disappeared instantly as he smacked my bottom and laughed. His men joined in the little joke. The apartment inside was as dilapidated as the outside of the building. We walked along a narrow dingy corridor where the greyish-yellow wallpaper peeled from the damp walls. It was cold and I noticed a kitchen and a dirty bathroom to my right. We passed both rooms and at the end of the corridor, it opened up into a small lounge with a sofa and two armchairs. A small TV sat in the corner playing to itself.

Kupi shouted a name.

"Lule!"

Within seconds another door opened up to the lounge and a woman walked through. She smiled as she noticed Kupi and sidled up to him giving him a kiss on the cheek. He showed no response, no emotion and instead told her that he had someone for her to look after. She walked up to me and looked me up and down. I disliked her from that second. She was slim, about twenty-eight or twenty-nine years old with hard, evil features, slightly shorter than me with dark straight hair. She wore a little makeup but it could not disguise her true face. There were no soft delicate curves, everything had a sharp edge, her cheekbones, her nose and even her chin as she took my face in her hand and examined me like an animal I knew finally that I had been kidnapped and there was no escape. She smiled at Kupi and gave him another kiss. She said something to him but I missed it, such was my revulsion for her.

She turned to me and pointed to the room where she had come from.

"You will sleep in there tonight."

"But I don't want to sleep here I want to go home, I've done nothing wrong."

Lule gave a little smirk, ignored me, and Kupi spoke to her again, saying he would be back in the morning. Kupi left soon after along with two of his men leaving one guard armed with a machine gun. He appeared to be making himself a bed up on the sofa and Lule ordered me into the bedroom. Reluctantly I walked slowly into the room. It had a double bed with a grubby duvet and a small, white plastic bedside cabinet and nothing else. I studied the barred window that looked onto a busy street and thought about escape and yet we were so high up. Even the window was padlocked, I couldn't even shout for help. I burst into tears at the hopelessness of the situation trying to make sense of everything that had happened and wished I could have turned back the clock. I remembered Brian's last words. *Don't be going outside.* Why hadn't I listened to him for once?

Lule came into the room a little later and appeared to be ready for bed.

"What are you doing?" I asked.

She looked at me as if I was stupid.

"I'm going to bed," she said. "It's a one-bedroom apartment you stupid bitch and we're sharing this bed."

She shrugged her shoulders.

"Or you can take your chance on the sofa with Azem's guard, Naim."

"Who are you?" I asked. "What are you doing here? Are you Azem's wife?"

"Questions, questions," Lule replied shaking her head. "No, I'm not Azem's wife. I guess you could call me his mistress. He looks after me, feeds and clothes me and fucks me whenever he feels the need."

I had never heard a woman speak this way before, I was totally disgusted and I think Lule sensed it which encouraged her even more as she appeared to enjoy shocking me.

"Ahhh… the pretty little virgin, soon to be Azem's other whore and then he'll have two." She looked at me inquisitively.

"You really are a virgin."

I nodded.

"Well, well, isn't Azem the lucky one."

CHAPTER EIGHT
THE DEN OF INIQUITY

L ule and I slept together in the double bed that first night. Such was my distaste for her I turned my back on her. Within a few minutes, she was fast asleep and snoring like an old dog. I envied her sleeping so soundly and prayed that I would drift off too, but sleep wouldn't come. I wondered if Lule was a prisoner too, I hadn't asked her but I had noticed that when they had locked the apartment when Azem and his mob had left, it had been the guard they'd thrown the keys to and not Lule. Had I misjudged her? Was she in the same predicament I was? I didn't like the look of her but was there some justification in her attitude and hostility if she too had been locked up against her will for weeks or even months on end?

I replayed the events of the day in my head and Brian's words came to me again and again. I remember looking at my watch as midnight came and went and the time dragged by as I watched the small pointer creep past one and then two and three in the morning as the city fell silent. I couldn't quite believe I'd left my mobile phone in the apartment as I went for a magazine. It was very small and fitted quite easily into my pocket and perhaps there might have been an opportunity to call for help if Kupi and his gang had missed it. They certainly hadn't searched me and who knows, when they'd left me alone there might have been an opportunity to call Brian and tell him exactly what had happened. I'd even read somewhere that by leaving a mobile phone switched on the location could be pinpointed quite accurately. It was all incidental now as I pictured my phone sitting on a shelf by the front door of the apartment. I had looked at it and remembered thinking – *will I take it with me? Pointless*, I thought. *I'm only going for a magazine.*

There had been another power cut and there was no electricity in the apartment and at 4.10 a.m. I got an uncontrollable urge to pee. I was so frightened and didn't want to move. The thought of having to walk into the lounge and bypass Kupi's guard en route to the bathroom filled me with dread. These men had almost raped me and talked about it as if it was an almost regular occurrence and I ran the scenario through my head and pictured him waking as I disturbed him. I had a vision of the guard trapping me on the way back from the bathroom, pulling me down onto the sofa and overpowering me.

I paced the floor of the room for at least an hour until my bladder cried out *no more*. It was no good, I had to go and I opened the bedroom door as quietly as I could. To my relief, the lounge reverberated with more snoring from the sleeping guard. Although it was pitch black my eyes were well accustomed to the dark and thankfully I managed to negotiate the sparse furnishings and tip-toed silently past the sofa and made it to the bathroom without rousing him.

After I'd finished I instinctively reached behind me and nearly made the mistake of flushing the toilet. It was an old toilet and no doubt noisy and it could have been disastrous. My hand hovered on the toilet handle as I said a silent prayer of thanks to the almighty for stopping me when he did. So instead I left it unflushed and crept quietly back through the lounge, into the bedroom and slid back into bed. I managed to fall asleep after that but for no longer than an hour at the most and then I was awake again and the nightmare was back.

My watch told me it was just after twenty minutes past six. I lay wide awake as I watched the daylight gradually light up the small dingy room. It was an awful place. One table with makeup on and nothing more than a box room in need of a major overhaul. Some of the wallpaper near the ceiling was hanging off and the once-white paintwork was stained a dull nicotine yellow. It smelled of damp and cigarettes and body odour and there was an occasional but distinct waft of ammonia.

I told myself I should be shattered and I longed to fall asleep if only for an hour or two but the adrenalin coursing through my body would not allow it. I had been snatched from a street, beaten and abused and nearly raped and forced to spend a night in a building that was alien to me, sleeping with someone I loathed. I was cold and I felt dirty and as much as I wanted to sleep I knew it would not happen.

It was 8.30 am when Lule woke up. She looked around the room and focussed on her new bedmate as the events of the previous evening registered once again.

"Ahhh," she said, "why if it isn't our little virgin, Mother Teresa?"

Lule sat upright and twisted her legs over the bed as she sat for several seconds before standing. She reached for a packet on the cabinet, pulled out a cigarette, lit up and blew several plumes of smoke high into the air. She walked over to the window and looked down into the street below. It was a dull grey day and little droplets of rain fell against the windowpane that had a crack in the bottom right-hand corner.

"Another beautiful day in paradise," she said with a sigh and a shrug of the shoulders.

As she walked towards the bedroom door she turned and faced me.

"I think it's best if you stay in here Mother Teresa. You don't want to tempt that guard out there with your cute little untouched ass," she laughed out loud. "I'll bring you something to eat."

Lule returned about twenty minutes later. She brought me some bread with a small sachet of honey and some water.

"No electricity so no coffee and the bread is a couple of days old so it's a little hard. I'm sorry," she said, as she shrugged her shoulders in a way that said that's the best you're going to get.

I stayed in the room for the rest of the morning too petrified to move. I'd seen exactly what Naim was capable of as he was fully prepared to rape me before Kupi called him off. Lule was probably right; it was best to stay where I was, at least for the time being.

That first day was a blur as I nearly wore a hole in the bedroom carpet pacing back and forward. I stared out of the window a hundred times looking and imagining a way I could get out of there and escape. But it was impossible and I knew it. The window was padlocked and barred and even if by a miracle I could have overcome those obstacles I was several storeys up and as far as I could see there was no fire escape in which to get down to ground level. I thought of a way to break the window and shout for help. That was a possibility. The window pane was already broken and the leg of the bedside cabinet could certainly complete the task. And yet would I even be heard above the noise of the traffic? It was quieter first thing in the morning but then again it was quieter because there was nobody around so would my screams and cries for help fall on deaf ears. I talked myself out of it. The guard, the vicious, brutal, bear of a man was less than ten metres away, it would take him no more than a few seconds to reach me and then what?

I thought back to yesterday when I'd looked into the kitchen. That window was barred too and I believe it looked onto a brick wall. I cast my mind back to the night before when I had to go to the bathroom. I think the bathroom was windowless. It was dark and yet my eyes took everything in and I couldn't remember a window, not even a small one. I grew despondent as I realised that the kidnappers had obviously thought of these things. The front door was a classic example of how security conscious they were. The front entrance was the only real possibility of getting out of there and they had fitted an additional reinforced steel door that looked as if it had come from a high-security prison block. No, I would bide my time and wait for my chance of some other way to get out of there.

As the day progressed the thought of escape was never far away. I then began to think that they would eventually let me go because they would do a little investigating, check out my story and realise that I had been telling the truth. I convinced myself that although they had at first been very abusive and brutal, their attitudes would change once they knew I was telling the truth. That's why Kupi hadn't turned up today, he'd be out with his men, they would be talking to Brian and Peter and they'd confirm everything I'd said and they'd return soon and apologise and I'd be back by nightfall. They knew where Brian and Peter lived so it wouldn't be difficult to talk to them and needless to say Brian and Peter would realise that I had been taken and would answer any questions that would secure my imminent release.

The door opened and Lule breezed through with some cups of coffee.

"Drink this while you can," she said. "The electricity is back on so take something hot."

"Where is Azem?" I asked.

She placed the cups on the bedside cabinet.

"How the fuck should I know?"

"But he comes here most days?"

She shook her head.

"No, not really. He arranges a few meetings with his associates here and when he wants to be satisfied he comes to screw me but apart from that he's his own man. He has business to attend to and his wife and family, so I'm afraid my little virgin girl that he'll be back here when he's good and ready and not before."

She pointed to the coffee cup.

"So drink up and relax."

"Why are you so abusive to me?" I asked. "Why do you speak to me like this? I'm not your enemy. I'm a refugee, no more than that. I am not a spy or a whore, I'm a village girl from Veliki Trnovac and I haven't harmed you or anyone else and yet still you mock me."

I think I took Lule by surprise as she frowned and stuttered. I still hadn't figured out exactly what she was or who she was but I made a mental note that I would dig deep and find out exactly the type of girl she was.

Kupi didn't turn up that first evening either and I remember boredom was the biggest hurdle I had to overcome. There was a small television in the lounge and after some hours I plucked up a little courage and ventured out there. Naim sat on the sofa and Lule in another armchair as they concentrated on some pathetic game show and tried to answer the questions but although I so wanted to sit down and join them I kept looking at Naim and his perverted little grin as he looked me up and down and I couldn't bear to be in the same room as him. As I turned and walked away from him I somehow believed he had scored a small victory against me and I hated myself for allowing that to happen.

I lay on the bed studying the patterns of paint on the ceiling. There was nothing else much to do as I listened to the enthusiastic audience of the game show through the open bedroom door as they shouted encouragement to the contestants and I listened to Lule and Naim as they continued their private individual contest to see who could answer the most questions. I spent a lot of time praying. Although I didn't consider myself particularly religious, it's strange who you will turn to when the situation looks bleak. I talked to God and hoped that the sky wasn't empty.

Kupi turned up after three days. Later that evening I would find out exactly the type of girl Lule was and complimented myself on my good judge of character.

It was the noise of the keys and the barrels of the locks being turned that first startled me. I was sitting in the bedroom as usual when I heard the commotion and I heard Naim jump from his seat and his rapid footsteps on the threadbare carpet. Lule burst into the bedroom looking for some lipstick and a make-up bag.

"Quick," she shouted. "It's the Boss, he's here."

I lay on the bed trying to look calm and relaxed but all the while trembling inwardly because judging by the reactions of Lule and Naim I realised Azem Kupi was not so much respected but feared. Who was this man? As I studied Lule I recalled how calm she had been over the last few days and yet here she was running around like a headless chicken, almost panic-stricken.

I stayed on the bed for some minutes as I heard the voices from the lounge. There seemed to be a few different men there, voices I couldn't recognise. Lule came through to the bedroom.

"Come, help me make some coffee."

I followed her into the lounge and took a sharp intake of breath as I saw Kupi again. He sat at a table with another two men I hadn't seen before and he smiled as I made eye contact with him. Two of his henchmen who had been prepared to rape me were also there, standing in the corner trying their best to look mean which they achieved quite easily. I followed on quickly behind Lule as we walked into the kitchen.

"Who are they?" I asked quietly. "What do they want, what are they doing here?"

Lule filled the kettle with water and ignored me.

"Get me half a dozen cups from the shelf and the coffee is over there."

I did as she asked.

"But why are they-"

"Hurry," she snapped at me, "Azem doesn't like to be kept waiting and stop asking so many fucking questions. You'll be better off if you just keep your mouth shut."

When the coffee was ready we carried the cups through to the lounge and placed them on the table. Kupi was clearly in some sort of meeting and for the most part ignored me and Lule. I walked back into the bedroom but kept the door open so that I could hear bits of the conversation. It all seemed to revolve around money and Kupi and the other two men appeared to be haggling over the price of something. The figures were quite high and always in US Dollars. I heard thirty thousand and as much as forty thousand and then they talked about commissions and percentages and even expenses.

I eventually got bored as the negotiations seemed to be going round in circles. I got up and stared out of the window again wondering how close I was to Brian and Peter. I didn't know Pristina that well and wished I had taken more notice of my surroundings when we had ventured out. It was a huge city, with nearly half a million residents I was led to believe and I began to feel depressed at the sheer scale of the place. I hated it and longed to be back with my parents in Veliki Trnovac. As the tears started to well up in my eyes again I wondered what would be going through the heads of Brian and Peter at that very moment. Would they be looking for me or would they be on their normal tour of duty? What would I be doing in their situation? I liked to think that our intimate moment meant more to Brian than I suspected and he'd be pulling out all the stops to look for me. Surely someone on that street the day I was kidnapped had taken notice of the car and the number plate and surely that car could be traced back to Kupi?

There was hope. There was always a little hope. I missed my American friends so much.

At that moment Lule appeared in the bedroom and she noticed my tears.

"What's the matter?" she asked.

Without thinking I replied.

"I miss my American friends. They were so kind to me."

It was the first thing that came into my head but it was a slip-up that Lule latched

on to. She walked back out of the room straight away and I heard her relay my words to Kupi. Lule was laughing, mimicking my accent and miming me. Kupi walked into the room, he had a strange look on his face.

"I'm nearly finished with this little bit of business," he said, "then we'll have a little fun because I hear you're missing your American friends."

I was shaking my head trying to protest as the scenarios flashed in front of me of just what Kupi meant by having fun. Lule stood behind him grinning like an idiot. It was clear she knew exactly what Kupi had in mind and she was going to enjoy every second. Kupi walked over to where I stood and reached behind me squeezing my backside hard.

"Don't worry," he said, "I'll help you get over your dear American friends."

I was shaking all over. Terrified at what was about to come my way and wished I could have taken those words back. Lule still stood in the doorway smoking a cigarette as Kupi brushed past her and walked back to the table.

The meeting was over all too soon and I heard the men leaving and bidding Kupi goodbye. I heard more conversations between him and his men and then they left too. Each time I heard the heavy steel door being slammed and locked it was as if it was somehow taunting me, telling me there was no means of escape.

Within minutes Kupi and Lule walked into the bedroom and Kupi locked the door behind him. I knew exactly what was on their minds as I begged them to open the door and let me out.

Lule was laughing as she slowly began to unbutton her dress and Kupi too, started to take his sweatshirt off.

"It's very boring waiting in here day after day," he said, "don't you think?"

I was crying, begging him to stop.

"We need a little excitement to brighten up the day?"

Lule was sitting on the bed and had removed her bra exposing her breasts. Kupi unbuckled his belt and dropped his trousers to the floor. He looked over to Lule and pointed his finger at her and then to his groin region.

"Show our little virgin how to pleasure a man with a mouth."

Lule didn't need to be told a second time. As she stood up she quickly removed her skirt and then her knickers and stood completely naked in front of Kupi before dropping to her knees.

"Please," I begged, "please let me go, I really don't want to do this."

I was crying and the more tears that fell the more it seemed to excite them. Lule moved forward and reached into Kupi's underpants. I covered my eyes with my hands.

"Watch," Kupi screamed at me, "watch what she does or it will be you who takes her place."

Lule was revelling in it, clearly enjoying my discomfort as she took Kupi's erect penis in her mouth and began sucking him aggressively as he placed his hands behind her head and began to moan. I had never seen anything like it before; I had never even seen a pornographic movie and the whole spectacle made me feel physically sick.

Kupi opened his eyes and looked over.

"You keep watching or there'll be fucking trouble. You keep watching and then you can copy her."

"Please no, don't make me do this."

"Don't worry," said Kupi, "you'll enjoy it I promise."

Lule pulled her head away and spoke.

"Come, virgin girl, come and join us."

Kupi slapped her across the head and she returned to what she had been doing as he looked over to me and grinned. He spoke softly.

"Are you watching bitch, are you watching carefully?"

Suddenly it appeared Kupi had other ideas as he pulled Lule from the floor and almost threw her onto the bed. He was red in the face and breathing hard. He turned to me again.

"You keep watching do you hear?"

I nodded like a trained dog but almost immediately I somehow realised that Kupi would possibly not last long enough to involve me in any of his depraved sex games. He appeared anxious and preoccupied with Lule, almost in a rush as he tore his underpants off, spread Lule's legs open and jumped on her.

Lule let out a little squeal, which clearly excited him as his backside became a blur as he thrust and grunted his way to orgasm. It lasted no more than two or three minutes and it was by far the most disgusting, revolting thing I had ever seen. Kupi rolled off Lule as he lay panting on the bed. Lule reached for the cigarette packet once again and lit two cigarettes as she placed one between Kupi's lips. They wallowed there for some minutes like the dirty pigs that they were as I stood fixed to the spot not quite believing what I had been unfortunate enough to witness.

Kupi climbed from the bed as he reached for his trousers and dressed. He took the key from his pocket and walked towards the door.

As he passed me he turned and smiled.

"Next time it will be your turn."

CHAPTER NINE
WITNESSING PURE EVIL FIRST-HAND

Lule walked around with a smile on her face for most of the following day teasing and taunting me about what I had witnessed. This was not the introduction to sex I had envisaged. I expected a tender beautiful moment on my wedding night with the husband I loved but instead experienced the actions of two perverted monsters sharing an act which should have remained private, but worse than that, I realised that the majority of the pleasure had been derived from the fact that they had disgusted and terrified me in equal measures.

She goaded me and convinced me that it was only a matter of time before it would be my turn and whenever I walked through to the toilet or into the kitchen she would make a point of   bringing Naim into the conversation and once even suggested that he take my virginity there and then. I think she embarrassed even Naim. Naim was the youngest of the guards, about twenty-two years of age and certainly not as confident or cocky as the others.

As always I was relieved to make it back to the relative safety of the bedroom where I closed the door in an attempt to block out the horrors that lay beyond. I'd stand by the broken window for hours looking down onto the street below and thought, if only people in the city knew I was up here, knew I was being held prisoner for no reason then surely they would come and get me. I looked down in the forlorn hope I would see Brian and Peter searching for me and that somehow I could shout or throw something at them to tell them where I was. I thought constantly of escape, of some idea where I could get messages out to people and yet I didn't even know the name of the apartment block or the number of the apartment.

Over the next few days, I managed to sneak a pen into the bedroom as well as some paper and I was always on standby to write a message and break the glass and throw an ornament or something heavy out of the window with my message attached if I saw a policeman or a UN soldier. I knew that if my message fell into the wrong hands I would undoubtedly be killed. Judging from Kupi's conversations with his gang and his boasts and claims, his gang numbered many and I knew his influence in the city was vast. I wondered if I would ever have the courage to attempt anything remotely resembling an escape. There were times of determination when I sincerely believed I could at least try something.

"It can be done," I told myself over and over again, "find a way."

And yet the message, whatever it was going to be never made it onto the paper and in time I even lost the pen. But still, I would stand by that window and look down and hope that by some miracle I would see Brian and Peter and they would see me and they would come to my rescue somehow. I daydreamed about them breaking through the door and shooting Naim and Kupi and I would take a little revenge and slap Lule hard across the face while they held her. I hated myself for thinking that way.

As the days passed there was no sign of Kupi or his gang, just me, Lule and Naim. I was aware that Lule was free to come and go as she pleased which puzzled me because at first, I assumed she was a prisoner like me. I hated her even more when I discovered she was part of Kupi's gang too, there of her own free will. I had been right from the outset, the woman was positively evil.

Lule did the shopping and cooked meals for her and Naim as they sat at a table and dined together at least once a day. The smells coming from the kitchen were pleasant enough but not once was I asked to join them. After they were finished Lule would bring me a plate of bread, sometimes some cheese and now and again a suxhuk, a smoked sausage cooked in herbs. That was my diet for the three or four weeks I was there while Naim and Lule ate soup, pasta and rice, fish and meat and always plenty of fresh vegetables. I confess it didn't worry me too much as my appetite was none existent. I ate the bread to survive, nothing more and I wanted to survive because I was determined they would not kill me through starvation. I had a strange, almost terrible hunger to survive. At times I was almost ashamed of my determination.

As I undressed at night I could see that my flesh was hanging from my bones and I could even see the shape of my thigh bones protruding through my skin. I had to stay strong I told myself, just in case I ever got the chance to run and pledged one night that I would not send anything back to the kitchen from that moment onwards.

Lule made me wash the dishes and clean the apartment every day as she and Naim sat smoking in clouds of toxic smoke that eventually made it into my lungs and I ended up with a permanent cough. No matter how well I cleaned the apartment and how much cleaning fluid and aerosol spray I used, it seemed to have little effect and always had that horrible stale smell with an almost permanent yellow, greyish cloud of smoke that seemed to hang in the air a few centimetres below the mustard coloured ceiling.

There were periods when Lule came over as being quite pleasant. She'd venture into the bedroom with hot coffee and sit on the bed beside me and she'd start asking me questions about my family and what it was like in Serbia. I'd give her the same answers and then the real questions would start as she hid behind her false smile. She'd ask about the Americans and my political views and try to trip me up with questions about Albania and Kosovo. I knew exactly what her remit was and that was to try and befriend me and take me into her confidence so that I would disclose some information that would prove I was a Serbian agent after all. She was the worst interrogator ever and the worst actress in the whole of the Balkans and I could see right through her. But nevertheless, I answered her questions with the same answers I had given Kupi and his mob, time and time again.

At times Lule acted more like a man than a woman. Her hygiene left a lot to be desired and more often than not she'd leave the toilet unflushed and thought nothing of breaking wind loudly although only in front of me, never the men. I'd make a point of trying to wash every day even if it meant standing at the sink with a handful of wet tissues. Lule on the other hand would quite happily go five, six, seven days without a shower and at times as she passed me in the corridor or in the bedroom I would get an unpleasant whiff of the stench that hung over her like a shroud.

I only had one pair of knickers, as I was too frightened to ask for some more. I'd asked Lule just a few days into my captivity but she'd flatly refused to give me a spare pair and said I had to ask Kupi for anything extra I needed. That was never going to happen.

Whenever I spoke to Kupi I found myself speaking in a whisper. I couldn't quite explain it and at times I was very conscious of my soft voice. It was as if I was too frightened to upset him and the louder I spoke the more aggressive it would surely sound. When I spoke in a whisper to Kupi he generally responded likewise as I lived in fear of him raising his voice.

Looking back on my time spent with Kupi, his gang and of course Lule, I sincerely believe that they knew I was not a Serbian spy. They had possibly thought that in the beginning, but as time passed by and they interrogated me over and over again, sometimes brutally and sometimes gently like Lule tried to achieve, they would inevitably realise that I had to be telling the truth and did not fit the profile of the kind of girl who had been trained for that sort of thing. I clung to the hope that one day the truth would hit them. I suspected that happened quite soon into my internment and when it did, Kupi shrugged his shoulders and decided to make money from me instead. Releasing me was not a consideration that had ever crossed his mind.

I was dozing on the bed feeling weak and pretty tired. For eight, nine, ten days I had hardly slept at all and inevitably it was now catching up on me. I was going to bed quite early and sleeping right through until the morning and I would sometimes get the urge to return to bed early afternoon. Lule seemed quite happy with that and left me to clean up and wash the dishes in my own time. My mind was also a little more relaxed as I had thought the worst thoughts possible to the point where I could think them no more and I almost resigned myself to the fact I was going to be holed up in the apartment for some time. I began to try and think of the nice things back home and my family and summer walks in the mountains and consciously tried to push the wicked thoughts and the despair out of my head. I figured there were only so many things I could fill my head with and believed the more good things I could squeeze in there, the more bad things would be pushed out.

I told myself there had been no violence for some time, nothing since I had been forced to watch Kupi and Lule's sordid little sex show. I convinced myself that those days had ended.

How wrong could I have been, as one day the door to my room burst open and Kupi ordered me through to the lounge. I must have been sleeping deep because I hadn't heard anyone come through the doors and when I walked through the lounge seemed to be filled with people. I was still half asleep and took a while to take everything in. Lule sat with her legs crossed in the armchair smoking as usual while Naim stood by the window holding his rifle, almost standing to attention. The huge guard with the balding head and the big nose, who I now knew as Rexha, sat at the table holding some sort of baton that looked as if it had traces of blood on it. Two of the other guards were apparently wrestling in the middle of the floor while everyone looked on.

Kupi told me to sit with him at the table and as I rubbed my eyes and tried to focus, I realised that the two guards weren't in fact wrestling each other but instead, violently struggling to hold a young blond girl down.

"What …," I said, "what is going on?"

"Sit!" Kupi barked out. "This will be entertaining I promise you, I want you to see this."

Before I could utter another word one of Kupi's men knelt down and struck the poor girl several times in the face and around the head. She appeared to stop struggling.

Rexha laughed.

"Hah, that will put a stop to her little fight."

Kupi spoke too.

"Untie her. If she resists again hit her again but only harder."

"No!" I cried out. "What has she done?"

I instinctively stood but Kupi pulled me hard back into the seat. I tried to appeal to the better nature of Lule as I looked over to where she sat.

"Lule, please make them stop."

I was wasting my breath. Lule didn't even look up from what was unfolding in front of her. It was as if she hadn't even heard me.

The girl was clearly dazed and bleeding from her mouth which was covered in sticky tape. Another the guards ripped the tape from her mouth and her head banged off the floor. I could see she had her hands taped behind her back and the other guard was working on that, cutting it with a large knife. When all of the tape was removed they started ripping and cutting at her clothes and I knew exactly what was coming next as I covered my face with my hands. Kupi lunged at me and pulled my hands away.

"You watch I tell you." he screamed. "You watch or you'll be taking her place."

They clawed and ripped at her clothes as she whimpered and pleaded with them but within minutes the fight in her had clearly deserted her. One of the guards kicked her hard in the stomach and she gasped for breath as her tears mixed with the blood that now covered her face. They removed her coat and her skirt and a blouse as she tried in vain to cover her modesty.

I looked at Kupi.

"What has she done, why are you doing this?"

My questions fell on deaf ears and as I looked again the poor girl had been stripped completely naked as Rexha looked on shouting encouragement. The two men stood and began to remove their own clothes until they too were completely naked.

Kupi was smiling as he pointed to them.

"This is good. Watch them closely now and take it all in."

He smiled.

"Knowledge is a good thing, you'll see now why they've removed the tape from her mouth."

The girl was beaten some more, kicked about the back and the head as she lay defenceless on the floor until she resembled nothing more than a limp rag doll. She was putty in their hands as the two men lifted her onto her hands and knees. She offered no resistance as one of them forced her head onto the floor. The eldest of the guards knelt behind her forcing her backside into the air and as he penetrated her violently, he began laughing, thrusting in and out of her roughly as his colleague forced his penis between her lips and took his pleasure with her mouth. Kupi, Lule and the rest of the animals burst out into a spontaneous round of applause and I couldn't watch as I screwed my eyes tightly shut. Thankfully Kupi, Rexha and Lule were too preoccupied with events on the dirty stained carpet to even notice. I opened my eyes as someone let out a little cheer. Lule was grinning at the man kneeling behind the girl as he continued, his companion satisfied and clearly finished as he pulled his trousers on but still unable to take his eyes off proceedings. They looked on like a pack of animals as the second participant eventually climaxed and fell moaning onto his back while everyone in the room applauded. The poor girl collapsed onto her stomach and at that point, I was convinced she was actually unconscious.

The two men dressed while Rexha congratulated them.

"A fine display gentlemen," he said and mumbled something to Kupi.

I heard the words *pastrim etnik* which means ethnic cleansing, and my blood ran cold. What did they mean? Were they going to kill her?

I turned to Kupi.

"You're going to kill her?"

Kupi looked puzzled.

"Not at all, what makes you think that?"

"I heard …"

Kupi interrupted.

"I asked you to watch not listen. Make sure you do as I say from now on is that clear."

"Yes, Azem."

"Good."

He stood and walked over to where the girl lay.

"She's had her punishment now she can return to the street."

He looked at me.

"You can get back to your bedroom, I've some business to attend to."

I wanted to help the girl so much but Kupi wouldn't have it.

"She'll come round in an hour or two don't worry."

He pointed to the bedroom.

"I won't tell you again."

"Yes, Azem."

I lay on the bed and sobbed like a baby. As a small girl, I truly believed in monsters and now I knew it to be true. The monsters were alive and well and more than real and they were walking amongst us.

The nightmare had returned, it was by far the worst thing I had ever witnessed and although I felt for the girl, the one thing that stood out was Lule watching that terrible spectacle, not only watching but seemingly enjoying the show, revelling in the pain and humiliation the girl was suffering. She came into the bedroom soon after, looking for more cigarettes.

I couldn't help myself as I berated her.

"How could you watch such a thing? How could you sit there and say nothing?"

I didn't even get a reaction from her as she found her cigarettes, pulled one from the box and lit up.

"You are the most evil disgusting creature I have ever met," I said through gritted teeth. "How do you sleep at night?"

Lule stopped as she reached the door. She told me I was the lucky one, and said it could have

been me Azem had *thrown to the dogs*. I wanted to rush forward and attack her as I clenched my fists and stiffened up but I managed to control myself. And that night I had to lie with her once again as she snored and broke wind throughout the night. Once again sleep would not come to me until the early hours of the morning. In my head, I had the images of that poor, broken, degraded girl and the evil smile of the woman lying next to me.

CHAPTER TEN
A DEAL – SOLD TO
THE HIGHEST BIDDER

Azem Kupi strolled into the bedroom the following morning acting as if the events of the previous day hadn't happened. I woke as he leaned over the bed smiling, rousing both Lule and me with the remark that it was a beautiful morning and that we would be going out for the day.

Lule jumped out of bed quicker than I had seen her move for some time and greeted him with a kiss on the cheek. I thought it was so false and more than a little pathetic. He brushed her away, almost ignoring her as he stared at me for some time. I felt so very uncomfortable and had no intention of getting out of bed as he stood in the room. Lule announced she needed to go to the bathroom and thankfully Kupi followed after her. I jumped up quickly and pulled on my jeans. I noticed they were looking rather grubby and I was more than aware that my other clothes were starting to smell too. Lule had offered me a pair of her old, torn jeans but the thought of wearing anything she had worn repulsed me. But perhaps I would need to take up Lule's offer soon; otherwise, my clothes would fall to pieces.

They hadn't even been washed since I'd been held captive, as I had nothing else to put on. I sighed out loud and I asked myself the same old question as I wondered how long they would keep me there. I shook my head, ran my fingers through my hair and walked through to the lounge. I felt dirty and unkempt. Naim sat by the table. I asked him where Kupi was and he smiled and pointed to the bathroom. I listened and heard some banging and noises coming from Lule that made it fairly obvious what was going on. After a few minutes, Kupi reappeared grinning as he did up his belt buckle.

As he passed me he spoke.

"How I wished that was you in there Lurata. But business is business and you're worth a lot of money to me."

What was he talking about?

Kupi sat at the table with Naim and they started to talk. I don't know where the courage came from but the words just seemed to tumble out of my mouth.

"What did you mean by that?"

They looked at each other and the two of them both grinned.

"Get me a coffee," he said, "I'll tell you when I'm good and ready when the deal has been arranged."

"What deal?" I asked as I stood with my hands on my hips trying to look determined.

"Coffee," he said quietly, "then perhaps we can talk."

I sat at the table with Kupi and Naim with three cups of steaming hot coffee. Kupi had almost drained his cup before he even looked at me.

"So what do you want to know?"

"I want to know what you meant by business being business."

Kupi looked at Naim again and I could see that whatever they were talking about had been discussed before.

Kupi took me by the hand and spoke softly but he spoke in a patronising manner.

"Have you heard of trafficking?"

I shook my head.

"I thought not," he said. "You've led a sheltered little existence so let me explain."

Kupi educated me in the next ten minutes. He told me about the sex trade and the prostitutes and the brothels that he and his gang controlled in Pristina and the surrounding areas. I listened in horror as he explained that the brothels were 'small change' and that the prostitutes walking the streets of Pristina were nothing but trouble and always looking to cheat him. Kupi spoke quite passionately about how he protected them and how they abused that trust. I was astonished at his attitude, as if these girls truly belonged to him as if he had every right to exploit them and take their money. He said that he was always punishing them but they would never learn. I couldn't believe what I was hearing.

"Once a street whore always a street whore," He said.

I wondered if the girl who had been raped and beaten the other day was one of Kupi's street girls. He said he was tired of them and that putting the problem onto someone else by selling the girls was the easiest option.

"You sell them?" I asked.

"Yes," Kupi said, "I am tired of them, it's far easier to sell them on."

"But how can you sell a girl that doesn't belong to you?" I asked naively. "How can you sell a human being at all?"

Kupi leaned forward and spoke in a whisper.

"But they do belong to me Lurata. Just like you."

I stood up angrily.

"I belong to no one."

Kupi looked at Naim and they both laughed, then he lunged at me and grabbed me by the hair forcing me back onto the seat.

"Just who the fuck do you think you are?" he spat. "So who do you think you belong to? The Americans? Your parents? No one has come to look for you have they? No one gives a fuck about you."

"Please Azem you are hurting me."

He had changed in an instant as he snarled at me.

"You're my bitch and don't forget it and yes, I'm going to sell you too, because you are a sweet innocent little virgin girl and there are plenty of rich men out there who are only happy to pay out a small fortune for someone like you."

I felt the tears welling up inside me as I started to shake.

"Sell me? You can't sell me I don't …"

Kupi slapped me hard across the face.

"You're not listening to me mother fucker."

He screamed as he pulled my face onto the table and held it there.

"You're my bitch and you're being sold, the deal is already done."

Kupi's words were haunting. I can still hear them to this day. *The deal is already done.* He released my hair and I lifted my head from the table as I stared at him. Then his persona changed. He smiled again, even stroking my face at one point. It was Jekyll and Hyde.

"Now, enough of this. We're going out for some lunch so you'll need to get ready."

"Lunch?"

What sort of sick game is he playing, I thought.

"Yes, I'm taking you to lunch with some friends, I told you earlier." He stood. "You need to get out of here for a little while, you've been here too long."

Kupi summoned Lule and instructed her to wash and dry my clothes. I went back into the bedroom and removed everything, as I stood naked before her.

"Great body," she said. "What a shame you are wasting it."

She told me they would be ready in an hour and I was so thankful that I would be wearing clean clothes again and more relieved that I wouldn't have to wear anything that had come into contact with her skin.

The next few hours were all rather bizarre. Lule brought me my clean clothes, all nicely pressed and I took a hot shower, applied a little make up and changed. I felt so refreshed and clean and actually realised that I was looking forward to going out. Kupi stood up as I walked into the lounge and looked me up and down as he threw me an approving type of look.

"Good," he said, "that's better."

He looked at Lule.

"Get her coat, it's bitterly cold out there and we don't want her to freeze."

Lule disappeared into the hallway and came back with two coats. Kupi told her that she wasn't coming. She was staying in the apartment with Naim. She was furious as she glared at me. She'd obviously assumed she would be coming too.

Kupi looked at his watch.

"Ten minutes," he said.

Sure enough in ten minutes time, there was more movement from the hallway and two of the guards walked into the apartment. Kupi threw me some car keys.

"Can you drive?" he said.

I nodded.

"Good. I'll tell you where to go once we get to the car."

The thought of escape was never far from my thoughts as we made our way down the stairs and into the street. I was immediately on the lookout for a policeman or a UN peacekeeper. I told myself I would take off and run to them. As if reading my mind Kupi spoke.

"Don't try anything stupid, we are all armed and one of us will shoot you dead on the spot."

As if to make a point he pulled his coat open to reveal the handle and stock of some sort of automatic machine gun that was small enough to be hidden in a large pocket that had been specially stitched in. But still, I looked hard at the pavements and the road praying that someone with a blue beret would somehow appear from nowhere. Despite the threat, I was ready to take a chance. I prayed that my will to escape was stronger than their desire to kill me.

One of Kupi's guards opened the driver's door and I climbed in and started the car. I couldn't help feeling that I had been somehow transported back to normality. I'd always loved driving and despite everything that had happened and what Kupi had said about selling me I genuinely enjoyed pushing the car into gear and pressing the accelerator to the floor and for a few delicious seconds I was free.

Kupi sat in the passenger seat and unbuttoned his coat so that I was always aware of the presence of his gun. The usual wisecracks came from the guards about female drivers as they joked about reverse parking. Kupi laughed each time and appeared to be quite relaxed. He told me to take the M2 out of the city and head towards Maxhunaj. The traffic was light and there was no sign of any NATO troops on the ground. I prayed under my breath that I would see a roadblock heavily policed. It was my only chance of escape, perhaps I could crash into it before Kupi and his gang could do anything about it and by the time they realised what was happening, armed police and soldiers would surround the vehicle. It was easy enough to plan the scenario in my head but I wondered if I could carry it out when it mattered.

But there were no roadblocks and no soldiers. Kupi had planned the route well. We passed through Vushtri and we drove another few kilometres then Kupi told me to turn to the left.

We followed a minor road for no more than half a mile and then looming up ahead was a large stone and wood building that turned out to be a restaurant specialising in pizzas. I pulled into the neat car park and we all got out. Kupi hadn't been lying, it did look as if we were going for lunch and I wondered if this was my opportunity to escape. Lunchtime meant there were many vehicles in the car park and I dared to hope that there would be some hungry police officers or soldiers who just happened to have decided to eat there too.

But I would be disappointed. The restaurant was full of men but not one of them wore a uniform. There were no women or girls, except for the waitresses who served the food and what was more alarming was that everyone seemed to know Azem Kupi and his gang. As we made our way to a pre-booked table on the far side of the restaurant, they greeted and acknowledged him, one or two even stood and offered a handshake. My hopes were dashed in an instant, this was Kupi's patch, his den, his lair, somewhere he felt safe and at home. It was exactly why he'd chosen to come here.

And so we ate pizza, delicious pizza and for a short period of time, my life took on an air of normality as we sat in a restaurant (albeit surrounded by Kupi's men) while waitresses passed pleasantries and brought us drinks and food.

But business was also on the agenda as towards the end of the meal another two men joined us. They appeared to be interested in me and one of them took a photograph with a small camera while Kupi kept looking at me much in the same way a proud father would look at his daughter. One of the men mentioned a doctor and a test and Kupi said they would not be disappointed.

Driving home I realised it all made perfect sense. He had taken me there to conclude the final piece of the transaction, to have proof that I truly existed and I knew exactly why they'd mentioned a doctor. This was more than common in Muslim society particularly the richer families of potential husbands-to-be. They had been talking about a virginity test.

The drive home was nothing more than a blur as everything fell into place and I realised that Kupi's outburst in the apartment was not a veiled threat but something that had been discussed, planned, brokered and implemented. I took the opportunity to look at Kupi on the drive home as he sat in the passenger seat. He looked as if he didn't have a care in the world. He looked like the cat that had just been handed the plate of cream.

As we drove into Pristina I didn't even bother to look for a policeman or a soldier. I was in despair, almost broken. By way of a celebration, Kupi took Lule into our bedroom again and they had sex. Needless to say, I was made to watch their depravity yet again. Lule asked me time and time again to join in the fun but for some reason, Kupi didn't. I took that to mean one thing. That he didn't want to be tempted into damaging the goods.

CHAPTER ELEVEN
DINING WITH THE MONSTERS

There was yet another rape in the apartment two days later. It wasn't quite so brutal as the earlier assault, the girl was much younger and she yielded far easier as she froze in fear and allowed Rexha to do as he wished. She resisted at first but almost from the outset, she could see that the odds were stacked against her with three more guards on standby as well as Kupi who all looked on. For a reason I couldn't understand, I was made to watch again but spent most of the time studying the evil reactions of Lule who oversaw proceedings with a real venomous pleasure and at one point even helped Rexha remove the girl's skirt. I remember the girl looking at her in disbelief. It was as if she could somehow comprehend the animalistic behaviour of the sergeant abusing her but not from the gentler sex. The girl lay on her back like a piece of cold meat while Rexha stripped off and climbed onto her. It was almost as if she'd resigned herself to her fate and although I could see in her face that she was terrified I admired her composure to a certain extent, it was almost as if she was saying let's get this over with.

Mercifully for the girl, Rexha didn't last long and he soon climbed off her. They threw her clothes at her and one of the guards bundled her towards the front door aggressively. There was a little commotion and some shouting at the door and I was aware of at least two or three blows and a squeal and some sobbing but the guard was back within a minute or two and I breathed a sigh of relief that her punishment had obviously been concluded and that she'd survived the experience. Even from the outset, from my first encounter with them, I sensed that these men were more than capable of killing and that life was cheap to them.

Kupi stood and buttoned up his jacket.

"Okay you," he said looking at me, "get your coat we're going out."

This time I sat in the back of the car with two guards on either side of me. Kupi sat in the passenger seat alongside the driver and I could see he was a little agitated, deep in thought while we once again drove beyond the city limits. I tried to take my bearings and carefully studied the road signs just in the off chance I somehow managed to get away. We headed to the west but didn't drive too far before Kupi turned round and announced it was lunchtime and that he was so hungry he could eat a bear.

The restaurant had been well chosen once again, well off the beaten track and somewhat more salubrious than the pizza restaurant. The waiters wore black bow ties and jackets and once again, to my dismay, everyone seemed to know Kupi and his gang. There was an overpowering stench of fish, really strong fish and it began to turn my stomach it was so bad. There were live crabs and lobsters in tanks and Kupi stood and studied one of them pointing to a large crustacean and passing comment to one of the waiters. We sat down and Kupi ordered some sort of special fish dish for the table. The waiter nodded in an approving manner and returned with some wine. I got the impression that Kupi was pushing the boat out, either trying to impress people or celebrating in some way.

Twenty minutes later there was a little movement by the door and Kupi stood. Some of the other diners also looked cautiously towards the door and two men walked over in the direction of our table. Kupi embraced them warmly while the other guards shook their hands. I had never seen them before. Kupi introduced them to me and I had no choice but to greet them. I expected a kiss from them that was the normal way a man greeted a female friend but the first man just shook my hand while the other gave me no more than a cursory nod.

The *special* arrived soon after, a huge pot of steaming fish casserole with potatoes and other vegetables and rice. The waiters brought more wine and of course plenty of bread and the men all tucked in as if they'd starved themselves for a month. It looked pleasant enough but the smell was overpowering and after what I had witnessed yet again in Kupi's apartment I had no appetite whatsoever. I recall watching Kupi eat like a hungry pig, and Rexha too, as if the morning's events had never taken place. They laughed and joked and gorged themselves. These men had no compassion as if they had somehow separated the evil and wickedness from the normality of sharing a meal with friends, an optical delusion of their consciousness. The poor girl and what they'd put her through hadn't even crossed their minds as they fed their fat bloated faces and within fifteen minutes the huge pot that graced the table was completely empty. What Pigs, I thought as my stomach turned in disgust.

Kupi and the two strangers (I never caught their names) excused themselves and walked off in the direction of the toilets. They were away for some time. When they returned Kupi ordered some fruit and some cheese and more bread and they gorged themselves some more.

I'd never seen men eat that way, not even during the huge celebrations after Ramadan where men had gone hungry for many days. And then they were away again, off to the toilets and I realised they were talking about a business that they did not want to share with me or the people in the restaurant. They brought more wine and then some brandy and by the time we all prepared to leave I realised that everyone was quite drunk and I wondered if this was perhaps my chance to take advantage of them. I looked over the table at Kupi who was staring at me and shaking his head and at that moment I was convinced that the man could actually read my mind.

We said our farewells to the strangers but I got the distinct feeling that it wouldn't be the last time I would see them.

As we left the restaurant the driver signalled to the right and I realised we were heading away from Pristina.

"Where are we going?" I asked. "This isn't the way back to the apartment."

Kupi turned around.

"We're going to Pejë," he said. "We're staying the night there."

"Why?" I asked.

Kupi looked at Rexha and the other guard sitting next to me and even though it was quite dark I caught a glimpse of his teeth... a smile.

"Because my dear little virgin girl, it's that little bit closer to Albania where you'll be spending the foreseeable future."

CHAPTER TWELVE
AZEM KUPI – A CHANGE OF
DIRECTION

"But why are you taking me to Albania? I don't want to go to Albania." I protested. "I want to go home to my family, please don't take me to Pejë. I just want to go home to my parents."

Kupi and his gang laughed at me. They laughed as I cried and they teased and taunted me all the way to Pejë. About four kilometres from the centre we stopped and Rexha, a guard and the driver got out. Once again Kupi told me to drive and he said goodbye to his men.

"What's happening?" I said. Where are they going, where are we going?"

"Drive," Kupi said, "they are staying here tonight."

He pointed up the street.

"Our apartment is a little nearer to the centre of Pejë.

"Our apartment? I don't understand."

He turned to me. His body language had changed and he was smiling at me, almost looking quite normal.

"Yes Lurata, our apartment... just the two of us. Just me and you."

It was my worst nightmare and my blood ran cold. I was going to be spending the night alone with Azem Kupi. He gave out instructions on where I should drive but my feet were trembling so much I could hardly keep them on the pedals and I even stalled the car at a red traffic light. I half expected Kupi to be angry but he wasn't. He spoke to me softly.

"Take your time Lurata, there's no hurry."

Kupi seemed to know a lot about the history of Pejë, he said that during World War II it had been occupied by Albania but then afterwards became part of Yugoslavia as part of the Kosovo province.

"There has always been tension here," he said. "Relations between Serbs and the majority of Albanians have always been strained during the whole of the 20th century."

He pointed to some of the buildings that were almost derelict. He explained that the Serbs had shelled them for many weeks.

"It's not a big city.," he said, "but the people are killing each other for fun and as for the buildings, destroying them has almost become a national pastime."

Soon after he pointed to an underground parking entrance and we drove inside. We took a lift to the sixth floor of an apartment block. It was totally different to the one I'd been kept prisoner in Pristina. There was no heavy steel security door just a normal wood-panelled door painted white with brass fixtures and a brass number 11 at eye level. Kupi produced a single key, opened the door and we walked in. He locked the door behind us and slipped the key back into his pocket. The apartment was quite pleasant, not what I expected and not what I had been used to and for once it didn't stink of tobacco. It was very modern and tastefully decorated with a large oblong-shaped lounge with soft sofas and a deep piled carpet. The curtains were drawn and Kupi switched on a couple of small lamps and then fiddled with a thermostat for the heating.

"Give it a few minutes it will soon heat up."

He took my coat and hung it on the back of a chair.

"Can I get you anything?" he asked politely.

"Like what?"

"A drink, as in a glass of wine, something stronger?"

"No thanks."

I was cold to the point of shivering and I wanted my coat back. I asked Kupi if I could make a coffee and he pointed me in the direction of the kitchen. Kupi was almost to the point of trusting me as if our relationship was not of a prisoner/captive but one of friends. I reminded myself I was very much still a prisoner and escape was uppermost in my thoughts, as always, as it had been from the very moment they had taken me.

I poured some water into the kettle and waited for it to boil all the while planning and thinking up a way of how I could get out of there. Kupi had had a lot of drinks. Perhaps I could encourage him to drink more and get him to fall asleep. He'd offered me wine, *something stronger* he'd said. I knew where he'd put the key and I could be out of there in seconds. I'd run for ten minutes, run as far and as fast as I could before starting

to look for a police station. It was possible. I looked in the
fridge, it was lightly stocked but there were some strong beers
and a bottle of white wine. In the corner of the kitchen was a
wine rack with three bottles of red. Red was Kupi's favourite. I
made him a coffee and also opened the wine and carried them
through on a tray.

He looked up and smiled. He was sitting on the sofa.

"Come and sit beside me Lurata."

I placed the tray on the table and poured him a glass of red
wine that I handed to him.

"There's coffee there too," I said pointing to the cup.

"Thanks."

He took the glass of wine and placed the rim to his lips. He
barely had a sip before he leaned over and placed the glass back
onto the tray. I'd need to be patient.

"Come and sit beside me," he repeated.

I did as he asked, I'd need to be nice to Kupi if I was going
to relax him and get him to drink more. I tried to calculate
exactly how much he'd had to drink. I counted at least half a
dozen beers and many glasses of wine during the meal and then
they'd started on brandy. My God, Kupi had drunk enough to
send a small army to sleep.

Kupi put his arm around me and pulled me in close.

"You're shivering," He said.

"I'm cold."

It wasn't the cold. I was trembling with fear. Although Kupi
had seemingly changed for the better I knew exactly what he was
capable of and I thought back to the first time I had encountered

him, when he'd punched and kicked and beat me and then ordered his guards to rape me. He pulled me closer. I could smell him, the aroma of the devil and I shook even more. My skin crawled, as if a thousand lice were picking at my skin. The plan, remember the plan.

I eased myself up.

"More wine Azem?"

I leaned forward and reached for his glass.

"No thanks, I'll stick to the coffee. I've had far too much to drink today and I'm a little tired."

Kupi stood and walked over to the TV, switched it on and settled for some sort of musical concert. As he walked back I asked him about his limp. How had that happened? Kupi told me he had suffered a gunshot wound in defence of Kosovo. He said he had been one of the founding members of the KLA.

"We started in February 1996," he said. "We attacked police stations and Yugoslav government officers who had killed Albanian civilians as part of an ethnic cleansing campaign. Of course, the Serbian authorities were quick to denounce the KLA as a terrorist organisation and reacted by increasing the number of security forces."

Kupi laughed.

"The silly bastards played right into our hands boosting our credibility overnight."

Kupi appeared very knowledgeable about the subject and told me how they flooded the area with Serb paramilitaries that prompted an exodus of Kosovan Albanians and of course a refugee crisis.

He turned to me.

"They started it so we must finish it."

Kupi said that people looked to him as a hero; they respected him greatly although he didn't like to talk about it too much. For a man of modesty, he talked for at least ten minutes about his exploits and his bravery and his courage. I'd given him the perfect platform to sell himself, to tell me what a great man he was and he seized the opportunity with both hands.

After he'd finished he reached for his wine glass and took a large mouthful. He looked at me and smiled and then he drained the glass.

He held out his hand.

"Come with me Lurata."

"Come with you?" I asked. "Where to?"

"Come with me to bed."

The involuntary shaking returned instantly.

"No Azem please."

"You do not want to be with me?"

"No Azem, it would be wrong. You know our culture, please understand."

Azem Kupi wasn't about to take no for an answer. I could see that the word of a woman

meant nothing to him. This was a man who was used to getting his own way and he reached for my hand and pulled me to my feet. He held me for some time staring into my eyes much in the same way Brian had before he kissed me. I turned my head away and pulled free. Azem's tender smile had gone as he took a step forward and reached for me again. He gently stroked my face.

"You are so very pretty," he said. "You'd be a perfect wife for a very lucky man."

What was Kupi up to? He'd already told me he was selling me, that the *deal was done*. I fought for breath as I felt myself being gently pulled towards the door on the far side of the lounge which I guessed was the bedroom.

I was right. Kupi reached for the door handle and located the light switch just inside the door. My gaze was fixed on a large king-sized bed. He had planned this all along. My emotions were in shreds as I tried to figure things out. He had been a changed man ever since we had left Rexha and the others on the other side of town. So, he wasn't going to sell me after all? And yet the virginity test, the mention of the medical men. What was going on?

Kupi pulled me into the bedroom and closed the door. I was thinking about where he'd left his jacket, the one with the front door key. He began to undress.

"Please Azem no."

He laid his shirt over a chair at the bottom of the bed.

"Don't you like me?"

I wanted to tell him I hated him with a passion, that he was vulgar and the vilest most violent beast I had ever encountered.

"Of course I like you Azem."

"Then lie with me, give yourself to me tonight," he said.

I started to sob, begging him again to understand our culture and that it was just not possible. Kupi was naked now and walked over to the bed. I could feel my heart pounding in my chest my muscles tightening by the second as he slipped under the blankets.

"Remove your clothes and come and join me."

This was the moment I had been dreading as soon as I realised that we would be spending the night alone. I somehow sensed that this was what Kupi had in mind. And yet it made no sense. What about the deal and the rich man who wanted to pay for a virgin?

"Please Azem no."

He frowned.

"We can do it the easy way or the hard way."

I find it difficult to describe how I felt at that moment. As teenage girls we would discuss our weddings and how beautiful and special they would be and when we got a little older we would also discuss those tender moments we would spend in the marital bed on our special night. It would be dreamy talk and we'd giggle and laugh and of course, some girls would claim to know more than others and stories that were only half true would be shared with each other. I imagined my wedding would be a grand affair, somewhere special and of course with a very handsome husband who would be kind and tender and I'd love him with all my heart as we shared that special moment together. And now as I slowly began to unbutton my blouse, those images in my head had been blown apart. Instead I was looking at a man I hated who was about to take that moment away from me and if I didn't yield to him voluntarily I knew he would initiate a vicious violent rape.

"Take it off."

I pulled my blouse over my shoulders and let it fall to the floor. He pointed to my bra.

"And that."

I knew my protests were futile now. Kupi was beyond the point of no return and I had to do exactly as he asked. I peeled off my bra and let that fall too. Kupi studied me for some time clearly excited at what he'd seen. He passed some comment but the words of the sentence did not register as I reached for the buckle of my belt and the tears I had been fighting for so long eventually came.

When I was completely naked I stood for some time pleading with Kupi to respect me. He repeated his words about doing it the hard or the easy way and told me it was my choice. Eventually I joined him under the sheets, sobbing hard. I turned my back on him and he wrapped his powerful arms around me as he kissed me on the back of the neck. My skin crawled as involuntary spasms coursed through me. Kupi asked me what was wrong and I told him I was cold. He squeezed at my breasts as he moaned with pleasure and his hands wandered all over me. He wrapped one of his arms tightly around the top of my thighs and pulled me hard into him. I could feel his erection pressing into my buttocks as he moved rhythmically back and forth as his groans grew louder.

He kept asking me to give myself to him and he kept asking me to turn around but as much as I feared the aggression that would no doubt come I just couldn't bring myself to face him. He was trying to force his penis between my legs from behind but I was determined that I wasn't going to make it easy for him and I sensed him getting more and more frustrated. And still he pushed against me, harder and more rapidly and I began to wonder when the inevitable rape would take place.

"Give yourself to me Lurata," he said time and time again but the more he said it the stiffer I became and I dared to think that the rape perhaps may not take place after all. Both hands cupped my breasts now and he rubbed his penis hard against my buttocks and I sensed that he was fast approaching his climax. It was an awful moment as he cried out loud and ejaculated and yet in many respects I was so relieved at the outcome. Kupi turned over and rolled away from me as I climbed from the bed.

"Where are you going?" he said.

"To the bathroom, I need to get cleaned up."

Kupi grunted and pulled the blankets up to his chin.

"You get back here quickly."

I walked through to the bathroom. The light was still on and I noticed Kupi's jacket slung across the back of the chair. I wouldn't be too hasty before retrieving the key. I would wait until he was sleeping.

I took a shower and washed Kupi from me. The water stream was powerful and I turned the shower up as hot as I could possibly bear it and scrubbed my whole body with a brush until it tingled. It was so different to the shower in the apartment in Pristina where we were lucky to get even lukewarm water for a few seconds. I stood for some minutes letting the water cascade over me. I told myself that every drip that disappeared through the plug in the bottom of the shower tray was a piece of Kupi as he had violated me. I felt strangely good, I was even a little pleased with myself that I'd somehow managed to avoid what I thought was the inevitable but then again I knew it wasn't over. I became aware of the door opening and looked over to see Kupi standing in the doorway. He stood and glared at me as I reached for the towel and stepped out of the cubicle.

"I told you to be quick," he said.

"Sorry," I replied, "the water is hot, it feels so good."

Kupi watched as I dressed and then turned and walked away. I followed him through to the bedroom. He was sitting up propped against a pillow and looked deep in thought.

"I wished you had given yourself to me," he said, "things could have been so different."

"What do you mean?" I asked.

I never got a reply as Kupi eased himself under the covers and closed his eyes. I got into bed beside him and turned my back. I looked at my illuminated watch display, it was just after midnight and remembered reading somewhere that around three in the morning was the time most people slept the deepest. I would lie awake and wait. I would wait for Kupi to sleep, to snore and then I would wait a little more. He was snoring gently within about fifteen minutes. Snoring had never sounded so good and I fought my natural desire to close my eyes.

I lost my battle somewhere between one and two in the morning and as Kupi woke me I looked at my watch and my heart sank as realisation set in that I'd slept most of the night. Kupi was telling me to get ready as we would soon be leaving. There was none of the tenderness in his voice that there had been the previous evening. He was back to his normal self, barking out orders and demanding a quick response. He spent some time on his mobile phone.

We were out of the apartment within twenty minutes and driving back out of the city of Pejë. Kupi hardly said a word and I thought it best to keep quiet myself. He had been quite cold towards me since he'd woken me.

The street we had driven into looked familiar and I realised it was where we'd dropped off Rexha and the other two guards. Kupi stopped the car and made a quick phone call on his mobile. Within a few minutes, Rexha and the two guards were walking up the street and coming towards the car. Kupi told me to get in the back and they made me sit in between two of the guards while Rexha climbed into the driver's seat and Kupi switched to the passenger side.

Kupi turned around to the two guards and nodded. They both produced a gun and made a point of showing me, then I got a gun barrel pressed on either side of my ribs.

"We are going to the border of Albania," He said. "If you try anything stupid they will shoot you dead."

CHAPTER THIRTEEN
SOLD TO THE HIGHEST BIDDER

We passed through the towns of Rastavica and then Junik and Kupi mumbled something to Rexha and pointed to a huge mountain up ahead.

Rexha turned to me.

"That is the mountain of Bjeshket e Nemuna and on the other side is Albania," he grinned wickedly. "That's your destination you Serb whore."

More than once I felt a gun barrel pressing into my ribs. Kupi was strangely quiet as he concentrated on the road up ahead.

"But I don't want to go to Albania Azem," I said.

He ignored me.

"Why are you taking me there?"

He turned.

"Didn't you hear him? So that your buyer can have some fun with you."

The car irrupted with the sound of laughter. It seemed everybody had to laugh at Kupi's jokes.

Bjeshket e Nemuna was drawing agonisingly close and I became aware that the men in the car took on a more sombre mood the nearer we got to the border but still I bombarded Kupi with questions that he chose to ignore.

Rexha took great pleasure in telling me that virgins were very much in demand. I had been told that before, but I would only be a virgin for a very short time and I was more concerned about what would happen to me afterwards.

"Azem… please talk to me. Will I be coming back soon?"

I had almost resigned myself to the fact I had been sold and accepted that a very rich man would want to take my virginity. I looked around the car at the animals I was travelling with. Surely the rich buyer couldn't be any worse than them.

"How long will I be there Azem?"

Rexha looked in the rearview mirror and I caught his eye.

"There are sixty-four positions in the book of the Kama sutra, so your buyer will fuck you at least sixty-four times before he tires of you and sends you back."

What's the Kama sutra? I asked myself.

"You will come and get me?"

My question remained unanswered.

"Please Azem tell me what-"

"Mother fucking whore," he snapped, "don't you ever shut up? I'll tell you what's going to happen. You've been sold to the highest bidder for a large sum of money but Rexha is correct, he'll be sick of you within the month and he'll be looking for another virgin girl to replace you and then you'll be sold for organ harvesting."

I'd never heard of organ harvesting.

"What's that?" I asked.

Kupi turned around as he spoke through gritted teeth.

"Mother fucker, I swear if you ask one more question I'll order those two beside you to put a bullet into your head."

Rexha pointed ahead.

"The border Boss. We are nearly there."

Kupi looked up.

"Okay," he said, "let's keep calm."

Sitting in the middle of the back seat I had a perfect view as we neared the border and I could see that there was a large queue of cars and buses and many UN vehicles blocking the road. Kupi and his men looked nervous and Rexha fidgeted and changed gear many times when there was no real need. Kupi slapped his wrist.

"Keep fucking calm I said."

I noticed that many cars were being turned around and just an odd one was being allowed through. Kupi and Rexha were anxious. Rexha said that it wasn't normal. As we neared the roadblock I recognised a flag on one of the soldiers' uniforms. He was Italian and I also noticed another Italian flag fluttering in the breeze from the aerial of a truck parked by the side of the road. There were men in other uniforms too and a police car. As if sensing what I was thinking one of the guards pushed the barrel of his gun into my kidneys. I let out a little yelp and Kupi turned around as he gave the guard an approving look.

"If she says one word don't hesitate to pull the trigger," he said, before turning back as he wound the window down.

A policeman approached the window with two Italian soldiers carrying rifles.

Kupi spoke politely to the policeman who turned out to be a police translator.

"What seems to be the problem officer?"

"The border is closed to anyone who doesn't live in Albania. Have you any ID that states that you live in Albania?"

"No," Kupi said. "We are from Kosovo but we need to get to Albania tonight for a friend's   funeral."

"No chance I'm afraid. You'll need to turn back."

Kupi tried to argue with him, nicely at first, he sounded rather persuasive.

"Whose decision is this?"

The policeman pointed to the Italian soldiers.

"The UN," he said. "I have no authority here, now please, turn around as quick as you can."

Kupi let out a sigh.

"But we can't, we have a funeral, you must appreciate how important it is to pay our last respects?"

One of the Italians leaned through the window and looked at me. I was so close to saying something but of course, I didn't know any Italian. What would I say? And then he disappeared, looking at the car behind us. Kupi had pulled out his wallet and opened it in front of the policeman. It was full of money and he pulled out a handful of US dollars.

"If it's a question of money I'm sure we can…"

The policeman turned aggressive and started shouting abuse, saying that we were lucky we all weren't arrested there and then. The policemen took Kupi's dollars and threw them back into his lap.

"Get going," he said. "Get your car turned around right this second or I'll have you all arrested. The border is closed and I won't tell you again."

Kupi was furious as Rexha performed a quick three-point turn and we headed back in the direction we had come from. He cursed and swore and banged his fist on the side of the door.

"Mother fucking Italian bastards, who do they think they are? This is my country, not theirs, the mother fuckers."

I had never seen Kupi in such a bad mood as Rexha tried to placate him and tell him they could come back in a day or two.

Kupi didn't seem to be listening. He turned towards me.

"It's her fucking fault, she's bad news, and She's causing me too much trouble."

Kupi rubbed at the side of his temples as he looked down at the floor and then he looked up as if he'd thought of something.

"Fuck the buyer, fuck him. He's not getting her."

Rexha looked at him.

"What do you mean Boss? She's worth a lot of money."

"Fuck him," Kupi repeated, "I'll rape her myself and then we'll harvest her."

I couldn't help myself.

"Harvest me? I don't understand. What does that mean?"

The guard to my left spoke grinning.

"Will I tell the bitch Boss?"

Kupi looked at the guard and then at me.

"I'll tell her. I'll tell the mother fucking Serbian bitch."

The car fell silent as Kupi spoke. It was as if he'd composed himself to deliver my sentence. He told me exactly what he meant by harvesting.

"It's all quite simple," he said, "we're becoming quite expert the more we do it. You'll be taken to one of our doctors and operated on, he'll test your blood beforehand so that he can assess your health and our contacts can find a match. Don't worry, the doctor will sedate you before he removes your heart, your liver and your kidneys too."

Kupi was rubbing his hands together and smiling. The frustration and anger evident in his contorted face just a few moments before had completely disappeared. He spoke softly in a controlled manner and I was left in no doubt that this was no fairy story.

"We sell the organs to our black market contacts for up to forty thousand US dollars at a time."

Kupi let out a squeal of delight.

"Forty thousand dollars for one organ, can you believe that?"

He leaned over the front seat and ran a finger across my breasts, then all the way down to my navel.

"So you see, we don't need to whore you out because this little body is still worth a pretty packet."

Kupi repeated that he was going to rape me in Pristina and then let his men have some fun. Afterwards, he'd arrange the deal and by the end of the week, I'd be dead. I sat in the back of the car too stunned to move while the rest of the guards teased and ridiculed me, backing up Kupi's tale with stories of other young girls and Serb soldiers who had gone before me. A cold like I'd never experienced before washed over me. It started in my chest and moved slowly down my body into my stomach and my hips. I remember feeling as if someone was rubbing ice over my thighs as the feeling continued down to my ankles and finally into my toes. I felt numb   as if my blood had frozen solid. I couldn't move, I couldn't talk. I felt dead.

The two guards on either side of me were more aggressive than ever as Kupi sat smirking in the front while they described in great detail what they were going to do to me sexually. Their depravity knew no limits. These animals were the worst of the worst but I was now beyond fear and everything they said went in one ear and out the other. I was beyond caring.

Kupi was on the phone for the next twenty minutes and made no attempt to conceal or hide what he was discussing. He was brokering my deal, my death deal.

We drove back through Pejë, took a right turn in the centre of the city and headed out towards the east. After thirty or forty minutes Kupi announced he needed food. He told Rexha to look for a bar or a restaurant. Rexha said they were only ten minutes from a place called Kline.

"Perfect," Kupi said, "we'll have a little drink to celebrate our good fortune."

Rexha parked the car by the pavement as soon as we drove into Kline and I was pulled from the back door. The two guards flanked me while Kupi and Rexha walked on ahead in the direction of a small bar. We walked down three small steps to the bar that was just below ground level. When we got inside

Kupi was on his phone again. He stood against the bar and the barman placed a small beer in front of him.

"I really need to go to the toilet too," I said to the guards.

They ignored me and instead ushered me over to a table in the far corner. I watched Kupi and Rexha as they smoked and drank for some time. The barman brought a large jug of beer over to our table and a tin of coca cola, which I assumed was for me. As I opened the tin I looked over to the bar and spotted something that made me sit up straight. It was something familiar, a familiar face. He was not much older than me and stood at the opposite end of the bar to where Kupi and Rexha stood. I recognised him but from where? My heart was pounding in my chest as it came to me. I was more than familiar with him; he was from one of the small towns near Veliki Trnovac though I couldn't recall which one. I had seen him many times in one of the coffee bars back home. What was he doing in Kosovo? A refugee too perhaps? It didn't matter, it was a chance I told myself, a chance to get a message to him to call the police. I'd tell him and he'd recognise me too, realise there was something quite wrong by the look of fear on my face, the fact I'd lost so much weight since the last time he'd seen me.

"I really need to pee."

One of the guards leaned over the table.

"Go then, but remember I'm right behind you."

I stood up and walked away. The toilet was at the back of the bar and I would have to pass the man I recognized. I tried to take my time praying to myself that he would look in my direction. I stopped just a metre from him as I lingered and made a coughing noise. He looked up and saw me and a smile flicked across his face. He had recognized me. I returned his smile. Please call the police, I've been kidnapped I would say. I'd even prepared the exact words and then I'd walk away as soon as I'd said them.

"Please…"

I felt the familiar shape of the gun barrel sticking in my back.

"Move."

I stuttered nervously.

"I was asking where…"

"Fucking move now."

He pushed the gun harder into me and the sharp pain made me take a step forward. The man had to notice the desperation in my eyes, had to have spotted the gun or at least the aggression of the guard. I was so close, so close to getting my words out but each step closer to the toilet was another step further away from the man who could have summoned help. The guard followed me into the toilet and grabbed me by the throat.

"You stupid fucking bitch, I saw exactly what happened and Kupi did too."

"Please no, I didn't, I wasn't…"

He banged my head twice against the tiled wall, opened the door to the cubicle and shoved me in.

"I'm right here outside so do what you have to do and get out of there double quick."

I broke down in tears. I had been so close but hadn't managed to get my words out. I sat on the toilet sobbing my heart out. The guard was shouting at me to hurry and to keep quiet. I felt a tightening in my stomach and fell quickly to my knees as I felt my throat go into spasms and the taste of bile in my mouth as I vomited what little I had in my stomach into the toilet bowl.

"What's going on? Hurry up or I'll kick the fucking door in."

"Please… just give me a minute."

I could hear a commotion just outside the door and I could hear Kupi's voice. I pulled myself together and unlocked the door. The guard lunged at me and grabbed my hair as he pulled me out. I protested my innocence claiming I only wanted to ask the man where the toilet was. As I walked out of the toilet Kupi was waiting for me and slapped me hard across the face.

"I've heard what you did bitch. I'm sick of the trouble you are causing me."

I was aware of a voice, the barman was shouting something and I looked around for the familiar face but he had gone. The barman didn't look too happy. He was asking if everything was okay saying that he wasn't going to see girls hit in his bar. He stood beside Kupi while the guard stood behind him with two fingers pointing at his temple imitating a trigger action with his thumb. I knew he wouldn't hesitate to put a bullet in me and one in the barman if necessary.

"Is everything okay?" the barman asked.

Kupi's wallet was in his hand and he pulled out a fifty-dollar note, which he pressed into the barman's palm. It was his answer to everything as he told the barman to take his wife out at the weekend. The barman looked at me.

"Are you sure you're okay darling?"

I looked at Kupi and then at the guard, as time seemed to stand still. I wanted to run into the barman's arms and break down. I wanted to tell him everything these creatures had done to me, what they were going to do to me but I knew we would both end up dead. Kupi pulled out another fifty dollars and handed it to the man. The barman smiled and walked away.

Kupi snarled.

"And now you've cost me another hundred bucks."

Kupi guided me back to the table and sat alongside me. Rexha and the other guards sat there too as they ordered more beer. I couldn't quite comprehend the situation. They had taken me to the border with Albania where they'd planned to sell me and then Kupi had disclosed that I would be cut open, my organs removed and sold to the highest bidder and on top of that I'd been so close to executing an escape plan. And now they sat drinking beer and smoking as if the events of the past few hours hadn't even taken place.

I scoured the bar again, looking to see if my 'friend' had perhaps sat elsewhere or even wandered outside for a breath of fresh air. I waited and I waited as the men I sat with grew ever drunker. I ran a scenario through my head that my 'friend' had somehow read the hopelessness in my face and contacted the police because he suspected something wasn't quite right. I watched the door constantly. I tried to make eye contact with the barman thinking I could somehow mouth the word *help* to him but he never looked in my direction long enough. He seemed to be oblivious to the situation, probably planning a night out with his wife courtesy of Kupi's little gift.

It was dark outside now. We'd been in the bar for some hours. Just after nine o'clock Kupi's mobile rang and as he spoke his face turned to thunder. He glared at me with genuine hatred in his eyes and then he turned to Rexha.

"We're leaving now."

"But Boss," he said, "we've just ordered more beers, the night is young."

Kupi was already on his feet reaching for his bag.

"Now, we're going now."

The other two guards were under no illusion what Kupi meant by *now* and one of them had already lifted me up as we started walking towards the door. The barman noticed the mass exodus and shouted to Kupi that he hadn't paid his bill.

"Fuck you," Kupi said, "you've had enough money out of me today."

The barman looked for a second or two as if he was about to protest, to remonstrate with Kupi and his gang but then thought better of it. Before I had a chance to say anything to him I was out onto the street and being bundled into the car.

The snarl was back on Kupi's face as he shouted at me.

"You have done it this time," he said. "You are causing me more trouble by the hour."

"I don't know what you mean Azem," I said as I started to cry.

What had happened in there? Who was that phone call from and what had they said to make Kupi run so fast? He sat in the front talking to no one in particular cursing and complaining. I wondered had my friend indeed raised the alarm. Were the police on their way to the café and had someone somehow alerted Kupi to the fact? If so it was bad news, it meant Kupi had men on the police payroll too. Just how far had Kupi flung his net? He'd spoken of his time in the K.L.A. and yet he wore no uniform and I looked upon him as nothing more than a criminal. Now I wasn't so sure. Was his gang more powerful than I assumed?

I recognised the apartment block in Pristina straight away and my heart sank. I was heading back to that hell hole and the company of Lule and Naim.

Kupi barked out his instructions and the two guards on either side of me hauled me from the car. Kupi climbed out and told Rexha, who was driving, to wait five minutes. The four of us made our way up the stairs.

Kupi kept muttering something about trouble as he limped on ahead in front and the guards were being particularly aggressive and rough as we approached the familiar sight of the heavy steel door. Kupi fiddled with the key but he eventually opened it then opened the interior wooden door and walked in.

"Bring the bitch in," he said.

He lunged at me and grabbed me by the hair as he smacked me hard across the face.

"I wish I'd never set eyes on you, you bitch, you've been nothing but trouble from day one."

I was shaking my head in disbelief. Something had happened I told myself; something had to have happened to make him act this way. One minute he was sitting in a bar drinking and smoking and laughing with his friends and then that one phone call had changed everything.

Naim appeared. He told Kupi he had been to the toilet and said that Lule had gone shopping.

Kupi spoke to the guards, telling them to wait downstairs and as they left without questioning him he turned to me.

"It could have been so different and yet I now realise that you have been nothing but poison."

"But Azem, I haven't done anything, from the day you took me it's been you who has hurt me. I've never done anything to hurt you."

"Shut the fuck up," he said, "it's over do you hear."

I was aware of my stomach muscles tightening, the muscles in my throat contracting so much I could hardly speak. I knew something had happened, I sensed my time with Kupi was nearing an end and I feared it was an ending so horrific I didn't want to contemplate it.

"What do you mean Azem? What is over, what is going to happen to me?"

Kupi was on me in an instant as he grabbed my throat and squeezed hard lifting me onto my toes. He pointed to Naim.

"He's going to rape you and then he's going to kill you. That's what's going to happen."

I felt the breath draining from me as I gagged and struggled for air. My legs had turned to jelly and as Kupi released his grip I fell into a heap on the floor. Kupi kicked me full in the stomach and I squealed and burst into tears.

"Please Azem no. Please don't make him do that."

Kupi eased himself down onto the floor.

"He's going to fuck you stupid you little virgin and then he's going to kill you. How does that sound to you eh?"

Kupi taunted me as I begged him to let me live. He told me how the deal with my buyer had gone wrong and now I was *bad news* and he wouldn't even be able to broker a deal for my organs.

"So you're getting fucked and then killed."

He turned to Naim.

"Give me your gun."

"Please Azem," I begged.

Kupi seemed to study the gun and then handed it back to the guard.

You fuck her good and hard, you do anything you want to her and then put a pillow over her head to shoot her."

Naim was nodding.

"That way it will deaden the noise. Lule will help you with the body, wait until the early hours and put it in Lule's car."

I noticed that Naim didn't look to confident or too happy about the task he had been allocated but he was too scared to object.

"Where will I take the body Boss?"

Azem shrugged his shoulders.

"It doesn't matter, a bin or a skip. Leave it on the streets if you want and let the rats have their fill but make sure it's somewhere on the other side of town."

I was in pieces on the floor, crying harder than I had ever cried in my life.

I heard him tell Naim that he would pay with his life if anything went wrong and then Kupi stepped over me and was gone.

CHAPTER FOURTEEN
A CHANCE TO ESCAPE

Naim had that look in his eyes, the same look the guards had in theirs when Kupi had ordered them to rape me, which seemed such a long time ago now.

"Please Naim, don't do this to me."

Naim shrugged his shoulders.

"I have no choice Lurata, I'm a soldier following orders."

"But you…"

"You've no idea what the Boss is like? If I don't do this Kupi will kill me and he won't stop there, he'll torment and torture my family too."

I had misjudged Naim, he was the youngest and most inexperienced of the guards and never particularly aggressive towards me and I thought he was different. But I now knew he was more than capable of carrying out Kupi's instructions to the letter as he moved forward and stroked my hair.

"It has to be done," he said.

I felt the urge to pray. This was the end and I knew it and within a very short period of time, I felt as if all hope had drained away. I wanted to die but I didn't want to die in a violent aggressive way. Naim ran the palm of his hand across my breast.

"Let me pray Naim."

I told him to make it nice for me. I would give myself to him but I didn't want to be raped, I didn't want any violence.

"Make love to me before you kill me, make it nice for me Naim, don't abuse or mistreat me. This is my first time and I will give myself to you before you kill me."

Naim seemed to be taken by surprise but I persevered and begged him to make it nice. I told him it was the least I deserved and as long as he killed me Kupi would never need to know. Eventually, he came around to the idea and I prepared to give myself to him and then to die. Naim went through to the bedroom and came back with a cushion. He looked almost apologetic as he explained that he would kill me as soon as the sexual act had taken place.

I begged him not to leave me for the rats and he agreed.

"I must purify myself before I take you," he said. "I will wash and you must prepare yourself."

As Naim disappeared into the bathroom I fell to my knees and prayed. I told God I would accept whatever fate he had chosen for me, saying I was prepared to meet my maker. I had my head on the floor as I heard water running in the bathroom. It wouldn't be long now.

I still had my head on the floor when it came to me. Just before Naim had gone into the bathroom I had heard the sound of metal or steel being dropped lightly onto a table. What had I heard? I stood up slowly. I had heard keys. That was the sound I'd heard, a key or two on a key ring, no more. I had heard the sound a hundred times as my father had returned from work and laid his car keys on the table beside the front door. My tears somehow miraculously dried up as I dared to hope again. Surely Naim couldn't have been that stupid?

I walked over towards the door to the bathroom. There was a small table situated between the bathroom and the front door and as my eyes fell on the shiny surface I detected a glint of something shiny, something metal. It was still rather dingy as I walked towards the table and as my eyes grew accustomed to the surroundings and the light, they focussed on the two keys I had seen numerous guards and Kupi use to open the doors that had imprisoned me for so long. I froze in sheer panic for several seconds not knowing what to do. Surely it couldn't be this easy? I was trembling and I could feel my teeth chattering even though I wasn't particularly cold. I heard the water stop, the familiar rattle of the towel being pulled from the wooden towel rail.

I looked down at the table again. My God! He had left his gun there too. I stood staring at the keys and the gun and wondered what to do. I had never fired a gun in my life so took the decision to leave it where it was. I lifted the keys ever so gently from the table and congratulated myself that they hadn't made a sound. I crept towards the door wondering which key was for which door. Naim was whistling and I sensed he was nearly dry and would be out of the bathroom in seconds. There were two keys, one of them quite large and I convinced myself that it had to be for the big steel exterior door. The other key was more in keeping with a standard apartment door and I prayed to myself that I had made the right choice because I knew I wouldn't have the luxury of spare time. I could hardly hold the key as I was shaking so much and then I cursed to myself as the tears welled up in my eyes and I began to weep. *Stop it!* I told myself. *Stop crying.* I was so close. They were tears of expectancy. Was I going to make it out of there?

Naim had to be coming from the bathroom any second and would walk towards the lounge and realise I wasn't there and then he'd run towards the door and he'd catch me. He would be angry and he would rape me, probably there and then and then drag me through to the lounge to complete Kupi's orders.

I reached the door and held the smaller key to the opening of the lock and pushed. It slipped in like a warm knife in butter and I held my breath as I turned it quickly and the lock released. I pulled the door towards me and rested it gently on the wall as I fumbled for the large key. I heard footsteps behind me and looked over my shoulder as I saw Naim walking away from me towards the lounge. I had no more than thirty seconds. Shit! My hands were sweating, the key felt as if it was covered in olive oil but eventually, I managed to get it into the lock. I tried to turn it anti-clockwise but it wouldn't budge. Shit shit shit! I was so close, why wouldn't it turn?

I heard Naim calling.

"Lurata where are you?"

I twisted my hand clockwise and the key turned as the lock sprang open with a deafening clunk.

"Hey!"

Naim sprinted down the narrow corridor as I threw the heavy door against the wall and broke free. Naim was right behind me but I ran for my life in the direction of the stairs to the left. I almost fell down the first flight as I ran faster than I had ever run in my life. The decisions I had or rather hadn't made flashed through my head. Why hadn't I picked up his gun? Why hadn't I closed the door and locked it behind me? Silly decisions, wrong decisions, decisions that could cost me my life. I threw myself down the next flight of stairs, jumping from halfway and clearing six or seven stairs at a time but even then I could hear that Naim was closing in on me. I was almost in a daze as my body seemed to operate on automatic pilot and the only thoughts in my head were that I had to survive so that I could tell my parents everything that had happened to me. If I died soon after that, then that was okay but I couldn't die right now.

He was shouting.

"You fucking bitch, you won't get away from me."

We were two flights from the bottom and his screams and curses grew ever louder as he got nearer and nearer. He made a lunge at me over the stair rail as I turned into the last flight of stairs and I felt his fingers drag through my ponytail and he cursed as he slipped on the bend and his fingers caught nothing but fresh air. I could see the door to the front street but Naim was on me like a leech as I felt his hand on my shoulder. I managed to push the door open but I knew it was over, all Naim had to do was pull me back and he had me. He was young and strong, well built and well nourished and I was skin and bones and as weak as a kitten. As much as I fought him I knew it was over. It was at that moment Naim made another fateful, silly decision. He decided to punch me. Such was his temper, his anger at what I'd dared to do, he couldn't control himself and he spun me around and punched me as hard as he could. He caught me on the side of the cheek and he hit me so hard he lifted me off my feet and I flew bodily through the air. I cleared the pavement and landed in the middle of the street. I heard a screech of tyres behind me and although I was disorientated and on the verge of unconsciousness I was aware of a big jeep parked in the road. It was dark and I noticed the red brake lights shining underneath from the rear. I wanted to close my eyes and drift off into another place but I fought the feeling and raised myself to my hands and knees. I stood up and focussed on the white bonnet and noticed the letters UN and to the right a small Italian flag.

Naim had punched me into the path of a UN jeep and I couldn't have been happier as I waved my hands in front of it and started shouting for help. The Italian soldier jumped out and I instinctively ran around the truck towards him. As I reached him I remember his uniform being similar to that of Brian and Peter but as I looked up I noticed the look of horror on the soldier's face. He was looking over my shoulder. He was looking at Naim… what was wrong? As soon as I had reached the truck door the gunshots started. I had never heard gunshots before except on the DVDs of the movies I had watched in my childhood and I instinctively threw myself to the ground as the bullets bounced off the bonnet. The soldier reached for me shouting something in Italian that was indecipherable as he dragged me behind the truck. He was yelling into a walkie-talkie as he fired shots from a pistol out of the open window. I don't know how long the shooting lasted but probably no more than a minute. People were screaming and running in all directions. I had pulled myself into the cab and for a second I looked over the top of the steering wheel to see Naim crouching in the doorway firing off shot after shot. I was aware of another lorry that had pulled into the street and then a white jeep and suddenly there seemed to be UN soldiers everywhere. The next time I looked up Naim was gone and as I flopped back in the seat of the Italian UN jeep, I dared to believe that perhaps it might be over.

I was weeping tears of joy and yet at the same time I was wary. There were policemen around the truck now and they were asking me questions in Albanian but I was too paranoid to reply to them because they sounded just like Kupi and his gang and it was in the back of my mind that the phone call Kupi took in the bar may have been from someone connected to the police.

It was the Italian soldier who had dragged me to safety who I listened to. He spoke a little Albanian and he said it was over. He spoke softly while everyone in the immediate vicinity seemed to be shouting or screaming. It was utter chaos and the street filled up with more police cars and UN vehicles than I'd ever seen in one place, with flashing blue lights everywhere.

Someone produced a blanket from somewhere and they wrapped it around me. I refused to get out of the Italian jeep so they gave us an escort to the police station. I hadn't a clue where the police station was or in which direction we travelled. Everything was a blur, a fog of blue lights and sirens.

There were people waiting for me when we arrived at the Police Station and I remember being quite happy that they seemed to be taking the shooting so seriously. I still hadn't told anyone about my kidnap or what I had been through. No one had even asked my name. The Italian soldier helped me from the vehicle and put his arm around me as he guided me into the police station. Almost immediately a lady appeared speaking Albanian and said she was the official police interpreter.

I looked at her suspiciously.

"Get away from me," I said.

Looking back on the incident I'm quite ashamed of myself for my attitude towards the interpreter who was only doing her job but her first words to me were spoken in Albanian with a Kosovo, Pristina dialect, exactly the same way Kupi and his gang had spoken and I was paranoid that somehow they were part of the same gang. Something inside me wouldn't allow me to trust her and it was impossible for me to relax.

The adrenalin was pumping through me. Unless you've been shot at and seen your life flash before you, it's impossible to describe that feeling. I was trembling and crying at the same time and a few minutes later the tears had dried and I felt calm, but all the while I watched and listened to every door that opened, studied every single person who entered the large room and I looked at everything and everyone with suspicion, I was almost welded to the seat I sat on.

"I need to pee," I said to a Kosovan female policewoman.

She was very nice and said the toilets were on the next floor up. I was too terrified to leave my seat.

I shook my head.

"I'm not going."

She shrugged her shoulders.

"There are no toilets down here I'm afraid."

So I peed myself there and then. I felt strangely safe in that huge room with so many people fussing around me. The last thing I wanted to do was go into a quiet environment where I could be kidnapped again. I raged at everyone, I cursed and swore at anyone who spoke Albanian and insisted that the Italian soldiers stayed with me. I wanted to die so much. I had escaped from them, I had beaten them and now I wanted to die. It would be such a sweet moment.

One Kosovo policeman spoke softer than everyone else. He was a little older than the rest and at one point he leaned over and touched my arm. I jumped about a metre in the air and that's when they noticed I'd peed myself. The policeman spoke to someone and they brought me a fresh blanket.

The policeman smiled and told me I could sit in my own pee for as long as I wanted. I remember looking into his eyes and laughing.

"You clean yourself up when you're good and ready and not before," he said. "I'll stay here with you all night if you want."

It was at that point I realised that the policeman who was now kneeling before me was almost certainly one of the good guys.

"You'll stay here all night with me?" I asked.

"Yes," he said, "as long as you want."

We sat in silence for some minutes before he spoke again.

"Who kidnapped you?"

I was puzzled. I had told no one I had been kidnapped.

"Who kidnapped you?" he repeated.

"Azem Kupi that's who."

The policeman looked as if he was about to burst into tears as he let out a deep sigh and buried his face in his hands.

"How did you know I'd been kidnapped?"

He reached for my hands and I let him hold them.

"You are the only survivor. I'm so glad we've found you. We know people have been going missing for months but we can't find anyone to testify against him."

He then leaned into me and hugged me and I let him. He cried, I cried some more and I wouldn't let go of him because for some reason I trusted him with my life.

Eventually, he persuaded me to get cleaned up and we went to an interview room. It was full of people taking notes and now I was happy to talk and tell them everything that had happened. It was strange like a huge weight had been lifted from me. When the interviews were over he gave me a case number in a little transparent plastic bag. He told me to call him whenever I was ready to tell them more.

Finally, he asked me where I wanted to go, did I have any family in Pristina? I thought for a moment. There was only one place I wanted to go.

"I have two American friends, they are UN peacekeepers."

I told the policeman I didn't know the address where they stayed but gave him their full names. Within thirty minutes they had found them. The policeman said we would drive over there in the Italian truck and he would come with me himself.

I thanked him so much. I couldn't wait to see Brian and Peter. At last, my torment was over.

CHAPTER FIFTEEN
REUNITED WITH FRIENDS

I was trying to piece a timeline together and wondered how long I had been in the police station. I think I'd escaped at about midnight and it was now 4 a.m. The policeman had heard enough, taken enough statements and said I was finished for the time being, it was more than enough for one night he said and it was time to go. I had insisted that I would only travel back in a UN vehicle, I would not get in a Kosovan police car no matter how much I trusted the old policeman who had sat with me since I had arrived. The policeman was patient and sympathetic and said he understood, said he had called on the original two Italian soldiers who had rescued me. They would accompany me back along with a translator.

I remember staring at the clock for some time and eventually a policewoman announced that a car was outside waiting to take me to Brian and Peter. I recollect being upset that they had been woken at such an unsociable hour. The Italian soldiers greeted me with a handshake and I climbed into the back of a large jeep with the policeman and a translator. The translator leaned forward and directed the Italian driver through the deserted streets of Pristina until I started to recognise the buildings leading up to the apartment in the street where I had been originally captured. I started to panic a little as I began experiencing flashbacks but tried to compose myself and reassure myself that I would soon be safe.

As the jeep came to a stop at the very spot I had been kidnapped I broke down again. Everything came flooding back as if it was yesterday. The policeman put his strong arms around me and I buried myself into his heavy coat as the tears flowed again. I was shivering, I was so cold and tired too and yet it was a strange, tired feeling because I felt that if I succumbed to sleep I might never wake up again. My whole system was at breaking point and somehow I realised it. But I knew I needed to summon my last residues of energy just to make it to my feet.

The policeman shook me.

"Is that your friend?"

He said pointing to the doorway.

Peter stood in his pyjamas peering into the jeep.

"Yes," I said, "that's Peter."

It was raining but Peter came over to the jeep and I had an urge to run to him. The translator was the first out of the jeep and she began to explain in English exactly what had happened. Peter looked as if he wasn't listening to her. He just kept staring at me with a look of devastation written across his face.

I wondered where Brian was, why hadn't he come to meet me too?

"I'll take care of her," Peter said as he reached into the vehicle and took my hand.

I climbed out and he held me in his arms as he wept like a baby. Despite the heavy rain that was now falling we stood rooted to the spot for some minutes. The translator was still filling Peter in on everything that had happened to me and I heard Kupi's name several times. I looked over Peter's shoulder and noticed the old policeman looking on. He looked happy and seemed to approve of Peter and figured that I was in safe hands. We walked into the building locked together. Peter wouldn't let me go as he held me close to him. He opened the apartment door with one hand which seemed to take forever as he struggled with the keys in the locks. I wanted to tell him it would be easier with two hands but I knew he wouldn't let me go.

He took me straight into the kitchen where the small sofa I had slept on was still in the same place. He sat me down and we tried to have some sort of a conversation but as soon as I managed to blurt out half a dozen words I'd break down again and again. I couldn't stop crying, I felt so ashamed. Brian and Peter had warned me of the dangers in leaving the apartment, they'd told me a hundred times and yet I genuinely hadn't known just what lay outside the four walls otherwise I'd never have ventured out. Peter was trying to calm me down and all I could do was to keep apologising. I kept looking over towards the kitchen door expecting Brian to appear at any moment but it never happened. Perhaps Peter was on his own now, perhaps Brian had a girl in his room and thought it wasn't right to make an appearance at this time?

"You need a shower or a bath," Peter said, "you're cold and wet."

I nodded and I stood and Peter guided me towards the bathroom. There was a bath in there and Peter started to fill it. I recall the steam rising up from the water as it gradually filled while he was saying something about the power cuts being few and far between at the moment. Peter started to undress me. I didn't have the energy and sat there like a child being undressed for bath night by her mother. Peter stripped me down to my bra and panties and bizarrely left them on me as he lifted me into the warm water.

Peter washed me all over. He washed my hands and massaged my back with hot soapy water and then he washed and rinsed my hair. He washed me until the water was turning cold and then he filled it with more hot water but eventually, as my skin started to crease and wrinkle, he lifted me out and towelled me dry. He brought me a pair of his pyjamas and left me to change. He then came back with a pair of his slippers, three sizes too big, in the shape of ducks. They were yellow in colour and he slipped them onto my feet. We both laughed and then once again he took me in his arms and hugged me tight. We slid onto the bathroom floor and I sat in his lap. I fell asleep in Peter's arms. I fell into a deep, deep sleep and I slept better than I had slept in months.

When I awoke I was on the sofa in the lounge. It was daylight, perhaps mid-morning and I was still in Peter's arms. I could hear someone in the bathroom.

"Who's that?" I asked.

Peter frowned.

"Brian, who did you think it was?"

I remember being disappointed that it was Brian. Why hadn't he come to see me? I looked at the clock on the wall. It was nearly 10.30 am. I had been there for hours and it was as if Brian was ignoring me.

Peter looked nervous as if he had something to say. I asked him what was bothering him.

"It's that clear?" he said.

"Yes."

"The thing is you can't stay here Lurata, we have to work. Things have changed. You can't spend one more night here. It's not safe for you and it's not safe for us."

As Peter's words sank in Brian walked from the bathroom. He looked at me, gave a half smile and started to shake his head. At one point I thought he was going to walk away but he didn't. He walked over slowly and I stood to greet him. He took me in his arms for a split second and gave me a token hug. He was so cold towards me and as we broke apart he turned around and walked back into his bedroom. I felt so hurt... rejected... disappointed and I remember feeling sorry for myself. I remember thinking that after everything I had been through I didn't deserve this from my friends.

Peter repeated that they had to go to work and now that it was known that I had been brought back to the apartment it was impossible to stay there on my own. I wasn't stupid, I knew that, and yet I couldn't help feeling that Brian and Peter couldn't wait to get rid of me. He told me I couldn't stay in Pristina because they would be looking for me. He looked genuinely upset, saying that if it were possible he'd stay with me for 24 hours a day and take care of me but it wasn't.

I was annoyed with myself. I hadn't been thinking when the people at the police station had asked me where I wanted to go. What a stupid suggestion asking to come back here. No, I needed to get out of Pristina and I needed to get out of there quickly. I sensed Kupi and his gang were already making inroads as to my whereabouts and that they would already be hunting furiously for me. I had to be silenced, I had to be silenced like all the rest, this was what Peter was saying only he didn't quite have the bluntness to put it like that. I was on a death list. I had to be eliminated. According to the older policeman, I was the only living soul who could put Kupi and his gang behind bars for the rest of their lives. I needed to get out of Pristina quickly, across the border at least.

It was agreed that Peter and Brian would get me on a bus in the direction of Veliki Trnovac. By all accounts, the buses were running quite normally.

I wanted to say goodbye to the apartment, and I wandered from room to room in a daze, like a zombie. I stayed some time in the kitchen looking at my little bed where I had felt so safe and yet somehow knew I would never see it again. I felt sad, like a little girl lost; as if I were saying goodbye to a dying relative. I walked into Brian's room and picked up a CD cover.

Carlos Santana, Maria – Maria. I recalled how Brian had played the track almost constantly. The lyrics of one particular verse seemed to hang in the air as I hummed the tune and although Brian wasn't there, the aroma of his aftershave, Joop, seemed to permeate the room

You know you're my lover
When the wind blows
I can feel you through the weather
And even when we are apart
It still feels like we're together.

I wanted to cry, I wanted to hit out at someone or something, I wanted to smash the CD cover into pieces. I picked it up and held it above my head. That song meant so much to me or at least I thought it did. I was so close to throwing it onto the floor and putting the heel of my shoe through the plastic box. In the end, I thought better of it and placed it back into its original position. I walked into Peter's room and the kitchen and then into the bathroom and even though I knew it was all rather childish I said goodbye to everything.

It was time to go. Peter gave me a small American flag and a picture of himself sitting on a motorcycle. He said it would remind me of him. He looked at his watch and said his shift would be starting in two hours so we had to get a move on.

Brian stood in the doorway as I walked towards the door.

"I think it's best if I stay here," he said.

He turned to Peter, almost blanking me.

"I'll wait for you here, don't be too long."

I was embarrassed. I couldn't think what I had done to upset this man so much. He stepped forward and gave me a hug. There was no feeling in it, so different to the last time he had held me in his arms.

As we drove to the bus station Peter emphasised the danger I was in and the need for me to get across the border as quickly as possible. My old mobile was still in the apartment and Peter had kept it fully charged. I had tried to contact my parents all day but for some reason, it wouldn't connect. I tried to think positively and tried to imagine the meeting with my parents later that day. Forget about Pristina and Kupi I told myself, forget about the Kosovan police and Brian and Peter too. Life would be back to normal in Veliki Trnovac. I reassured myself that there had been no power cuts and that the buses were operating smoothly. Things had changed, things had changed for the better and in a few hours I would be back home and reunited with my beautiful parents and I'd start my life over again. They'd cry tears of joy and happiness and my mother would throw a big party and every single member of the family would be invited. There'd be a feast with all the finest fish and meat and no doubt a big plate of *Sarma*, her favourite dish, the cabbage marinated in mincemeat and spices. I could almost smell it.

Peter had made me sit in the back of his car and told me to keep my head down. We pulled into the bus station and he asked me to wait in the back while he checked out the buses. I crouched down in the back so that my head was below the window level of the door.

Peter returned with good news. He said he had checked out a bus heading near to Veliki Trnovac. He'd paid the bus driver who would look after me, he said that the bus was almost full with families on their way to meet their relatives in Serbia. Peter said that he had a nice feeling about the bus and that there were no soldiers on board, no policemen and no groups of men.

He pointed at it.

"It leaves in fifteen minutes, I'll stay here until it drives away."

So we said our goodbyes in the back of the car. Peter exuded a warmth that Brian lacked, his tears falling freely and he didn't seem ashamed or bothered. We sat there for an age and eventually as the bus engine fired up he ushered me out of the car. I climbed on the bus and took my seat. As it pulled away from the bus station the images of my parents' faces filled my head and gradually a smile appeared across my face as the memories of the last few months dissolved away.

My nightmare was eventually over.

CHAPTER SIXTEEN
BACK HOME TO VELIKI TRNOVAC, AND AN UNEXPECTED WELCOME

Those beautiful images of my parents' faces kept fading and instead were replaced with the disappointment of Brian's attitude towards me and the realisation that it had appeared he couldn't wait to see the back of me. On reflection, I knew everything made sense but it didn't help to soften the blow of rejection. The translator had explained what I'd been through and I would have thought that my two American friends could have somehow persuaded their commanding officer to grant at least one or two days off and I could have told them my story face to face, apologised to them or tried to make it up to them in some way. Yet they hadn't even picked up the phone and tried to contact anyone back at their headquarters. I don't believe in coincidences and I believe that people wander in and out of your life for a reason. I felt sure that this was not the way it was meant to finish with Brian. Somehow, somewhere I would see him again and he'd explain everything. But right at that moment in time, it was hard to get over, difficult to see the bigger picture.

I tried to push my feelings of hurt and confusion to the back of my mind and as we got nearer to Veliki Trnovac it seemed to work. I tried my mobile phone again but there was still no answer, but I wasn't unduly concerned because Peter had told me that all nearby communications were in a hell of a mess. It seemed the rebels on both sides were only too happy to target and sabotage mobile phone masts even though it affected their own communications too.

I reflected on my Agi's smile, his infectious laugh, my mother's almost hallucinogenic smell and I so wanted to melt into her arms again.

We passed a sign that said we were only three kilometres from Kamenice and soon after, we arrived at the border into Serbia. It had taken no more than two hours and the security was almost non-existent. There were a few UN soldiers who stopped the bus, peered through the windows and then waved us on. I gave a sigh of relief. Was it too much to expect that things really were back to normal and people had stopped killing each other   and stopped hating their neighbours?

A little while later the driver called me forward and told me we would not be stopping in Veliki Trnovac but in a village close by called Turija. I knew Turija well and it was only a few kilometres from Veliki Trnovac. I told him that was fine. It was a small village of no more than three thousand people and I even began to look forward to the short walk around the mountain to my hometown. It would be a novelty to me. It had been too long since I had been able to walk as a free person.

The driver dropped me off on the highway on the edge of town, at a bus stop strangely named *white sand*. He said there was no need to drive into the village, as I was the only one going there. I wondered how much Peter had paid him over and above his normal wage. I thought he was a little cold towards me and it seemed as if he couldn't wait to get rid of me. I wasn't perturbed and said goodbye and thanked him politely as I almost jumped from the steps of the bus. It felt good to get my feet onto home soil. I had been in Kosovo far too long and I knew it wouldn't be long before I was back where I belonged. I slung my bag onto my shoulder and pulled up my coat collar against the cold as I looked up at my favourite mountain, Malë Ternovc, towering above me. I had never seen such a beautiful sight in my entire life. Spring was on its way and as I set off walking I was almost startled by the birdsong that echoed all around me. I couldn't think that I had heard any birds singing during my overlong stay in Pristina.

I walked fast with a spring in my step. There were very few people and not once did I see any sign of a policeman or an army uniform that suited me fine. I could hear the very faint sound of gunfire in the distance but wasn't unduly concerned as it seemed many kilometres away and as I spotted the turn-off to Veliki Trnovac I picked up my pace once again.

I stood outside the house I had grown up in and took everything in. I wanted to run through the gates and up to the front door and yet I wanted to linger a while and fill my lungs with the smell of the mountains and clean unpolluted air. I felt free. If anyone was to ask me how I felt that day as

I stood outside my family home I would have said free, that's the one word I would have used. I felt as free as the birds that had accompanied me on my journey from Turija. As I walked through the gates I tried my best not to think too hard about the bullet holes in the wall. I looked up and noticed a thin wisp of smoke coming from the chimney. My parents were in for such a surprise.

The front door was open which I thought was a little strange. It was still quite cold and it made no sense. Nevertheless, I walked through the door.

"Agi, Nani," I called out. "It's me, Lurata, I'm home."

I waited in silence for some time but there was no sound, no reaction. I walked through the lounge and noticed the dying but still glowing embers in the fireplace. As I walked into the kitchen I was further relieved to see the remnants of breakfast on the table. There were two dirty plates and three or four slices of bread and two cups. Although the cups were quite cold the bread appeared to be relatively fresh and I breathed a sigh of relief. I knew my parents were here. I sensed they were alive and well.

I made my way cautiously upstairs and checked the bedrooms one by one but there was no sign of them. I walked back downstairs and out into the yard. I stood looking at the house trying to work things out. The door had been open so they couldn't be far and I noticed that Agi's car was parked by the far side of the wall so they hadn't gone shopping or visiting.

There was only one place they could be and that was in the basement where we kept the winter supply of wood. It made sense. The fire burning in the grate needed to be fed as it was almost out. That's where they would be I convinced myself. It was a scene I was familiar with, my father with his arms stretched out in front of him while Nani placed as many logs as he could carry on his outstretched arms.

I walked around to the back of the house and opened the door to the basement. For some reason, I didn't call out but instead crept quietly down the half-dozen stone steps. I pushed open the interior door to the wood store and almost cried with relief as I locked eyes with my parents and cried out in joy as I took a few steps forward before collapsing in a heap in front of them.

But it was not the emotional meeting I had envisaged. There were no tears of joy or embracing, no hugs and kisses or outpouring of grief or relief. I had imagined something out of the movies, a scene that would reflect the fact my parents hadn't seen or heard from me in nearly two months, parents who I assumed had been notified by the police or the UN that I had gone missing in a war zone. No. Instead, my father berated me.

"You silly girl. Why have you come back here?"

He looked terrified and angry. I looked at my mother who was crying but they weren't tears of joy. Fear was written right across her face.

"Nani... Agi.... Aren't you pleased to see me?"

I pitched forward and they had no choice but to hold me. That's what I wanted more than anything. Their touch. I wanted to drink in their smell and for a few delicious seconds I experienced just that.

"You have to go Lurata, please," my mother said.

I looked at them.

"But I'm home. Didn't they tell you I was kidnapped by Azem Kupi?"

My parents looked confused and they ignored what I had said.

"You have to go," my father repeated, "the soldiers are still here and it's not safe. They have been here and they are watching and they still …"

We all looked up at the same time. It was the front gates being pushed open and clashed against the stonewall. It was a sound I'd heard a thousand times. A vehicle of some sort drove fast into the garden and screeched to a halt.

Mother burst into tears.

"We tried to tell you, it's not safe."

"The army," Agi said, "they're back again."

Agi was on his feet trying to take control of the situation as he told me to stay where I was. He walked up the stone steps to confront the soldiers. I listened in to the conversation and it was immediately clear exactly who they had come for.

"Where is your daughter?"

"She is not here."

"Do not lie to us old man, we have people watching this house."

"But she isn't here I tell you."

My father protested and I heard a slap or a punch and the sound of a body fall to the ground. My mother pulled me in closer and hugged me tight. She knew and I knew that I was about to be taken away again and we both knew we could do nothing about it. Outside there was lots of swearing and shouting while inside my mother just wanted to hold me, to stroke my hair and she hummed a little lullaby as if she was so happy to have her only child back in her arms once again. I wasn't particularly frightened as the two soldiers came down the stairs. Agi was behind them still protesting and a trickle of blood trailed from the corner of his eye down his right cheek.

He was still trying to save me.

"You have no right to take her."

One of the soldiers raised his weapon towards my father.

"We have every right old man, we are the Serbian military and we are in control here."

"You are no more military than I am," Agi said. "Look at you, you're a damn mess, no badges or name tags and I swear none of you have had a wash or a shave since last week."

He was right. Although they wore army uniforms and carried guns there was something different about them. They reminded me of the soldiers on the mountain the night Uncle Demir saved the village. *The long-haired, tattooed brigade* someone had called them. They swore and cursed as they stepped forward and pulled my mother's arms from me and dragged me to my feet.

"She's coming with us for questioning, she's been spying for the Kosovans."

I almost laughed at the irony of it all. I had been accused of spying for the Serbs by the Kosovans and now the Serbs were suggesting I'd spied for Kosovo.

But I had no fight left in me. I didn't care anymore. I had seen my parents alive, they were safe and they had seen me too. That was all that mattered at that moment in time. I managed to hand my mother the police case number from Pristina and also the policeman's card. I didn't know if she would contact him but at that point, I wasn't particularly bothered. Perhaps the soldiers would question me and let me go, either way, I didn't want them to get their hands on that information. I said goodbye to my parents and told them not to worry.

In many respects, it was easier being taken for the second time because at least my parents knew who had taken me and I had been taken from my home town. If it makes any sense I felt somehow more content... I no longer felt lost anymore. I was more than willing to die having been taken by the enemy everyone feared.

There were only two soldiers and they blindfolded me and pushed me into the back of a jeep. The doors slammed and they started the engine and drove fast through the gates. I didn't ask any questions as I feared it was the end. Within minutes the interior of the jeep was filled with choking cigarette smoke as the two soldiers chatted to themselves and ignored me. At that stage, I wasn't remotely interested in what they were saying to each other.

We drove through a few towns as I heard the noise of the traffic and then after about half an hour the vehicle climbed and turned onto a twisting, winding road for about another fifteen minutes. We were now in the mountains.

Eventually, we stopped and I was ordered out. It was so peaceful, so quiet. They told me to keep my blindfold on, saying it was for my own good and I was aware of being led into a building. They took my blindfold off once they had closed the door. My eyes grew accustomed to the surroundings and it looked like the inside of an old farm building. I immediately noticed how cold it was.

"You don't say much," one of the soldiers snarled.

I shrugged my shoulders and looked away from him.

"She'll talk soon enough," his colleague said.

We walked along a long corridor with dirty straw on the ground but although it was obviously made to store animals there was no smell of cattle or sheep and no noise either. At the end of the corridor was a door that they opened and we all went inside. It looked like a small office, a box room with a table and two plastic chairs. There was an ashtray in the middle of the table but nothing else in the room.

One of the soldiers pointed to the chair on the far side of the table.

"Sit down and make yourself comfortable," he said. "Your interrogation will begin soon."

CHAPTER SEVENTEEN
A PRISONER ONCE AGAIN

A dark-haired pot-bellied man walked into the room. He wore the same uniform as the others but was clearly a lot older and higher in rank as the two soldiers promptly came to attention. He acknowledged their respect for his rank as a sergeant, sat down at the table in the chair opposite me and pulled out a packet that he placed on the table. He reached across, took out a cigarette, lit it and eased back in the chair, as he appeared to study me for some time.

"So," he said, "you've been to Pristina."

I ignored him. It appeared to be a statement rather than a question.

"Why have you come back?"

I looked at him, wondering how much he knew about what I'd been through. A part of me wanted to ignore him and see what he had to say and yet another part of me said tell the truth again, even though that hadn't done me any good during my first interrogation at the hands of Kupi and his gang.

"We know you've been to Kosovo, why did you go there?"

I took a deep breath and spoke.

"It was my father's decision, he feared for my safety."

"Your safety?"

"Yes, the whole village had nearly been massacred, people were being shot on the streets of Veliki Trnovac and there were rumours of rape and torture."

I told him how my father had insisted I left and I told him that he'd taken me over the mountain and how I'd managed to catch a bus to Pristina. I mentioned my Uncle Demir and the money and he didn't seem shocked by this revelation. He was either a part of that group or he'd heard about it at least. The man took a drag on his cigarette as he took things in. Did he believe me? It was some minutes before he spoke again.

"Why Pristina? Why Kosovo?"

Answer him, I told myself, *answer him honestly and you will be back with your parents in a few short hours.*

"Isn't it obvious?" I said. "It was supposed to be a UN safe area."

He detected the sarcasm in my voice.

"Supposed to be?"

"Yes, my father sent me there because that's what he believed only it didn't turn out that way."

He gestured with his hands that I should continue and I decided to tell him about my ordeal. I mentioned the name of Azem Kupi and told them of my appalling treatment at the hands of his gang and told them about what Kupi had said about killing me and selling my organs. I watched him closely as I mentioned the organ harvesting and once again there was no reaction, no real look of surprise. He stubbed out his cigarette in the ashtray and deliberately blew the smoke across the table into my face.

"Who is your boss?"

"My boss?" I said. "I haven't got a boss. I was kidnapped by Azem Kupi and accused of being a Serb spy."

The sergeant burst out laughing.

"A Serb spy?"

"Yes, they held me for six weeks but I managed to escape."

He shook his head and repeated his question, this time with a more menacing look on his face.

"Stop fucking around with your lies and tell me who your boss is."

I told him I wasn't lying. I told him they could check my story with the Pristina Police and even quoted him the case number. The two soldiers were grinning now as one turned to the other.

"The silly bitch thinks we liaise with the Kosovan cops?"

The sergeant repeated the question again.

"Who is your boss, who are you working for?"

I shook my head. I didn't bother to answer him and knew exactly where his questions were heading. It was the same as Kupi's questioning - asking me the same questions over and over again and ignoring my answers. Surely they realised that the story was plausible and I'd given them a case number that I'm sure they somehow could have checked out.

"Please, let me go home to my parents, you're an intelligent man, you can see I'm no spy."

He repeated the question again and again. I repeated the same answers. I waited for the first blow which would surely come soon. He asked me about Kupi, and asked me to explain everything they had done to me. I dared to think that perhaps I was getting through to him and I enthusiastically took him through the timeline of events. He sat for at least five minutes in silence and then he stood.

He leaned over me.

"You're lying."

"No I'm not ..."

He slapped me hard across the face.

"You're fucking lying, your story is shit. You are one of their own and they wouldn't treat you like that."

It was a thought that had crossed my mind a hundred times and I could understand exactly why he thought that. It was true, I was an Albanian-speaking Muslim and they were too and they had treated me like an animal and he couldn't accept that.

I was crying.

"You're right, I couldn't believe it either, they spoke in the same tongue and we worshipped the same god but it made no difference. I swear it's all true."

The sergeant upended the table in a fit of rage.

"It's not possible," he screamed as the table the ashtray and his chair crashed onto the floor.

I was left sitting alone on the plastic seat.

"You're fucking lying."

He walked around the room for thirty seconds or so lashing out with his feet at the chair and on one occasion punched the wooden door so hard he left a large indentation in one of the panels. He walked over to his two soldiers who by now were standing on either side of the door. He whispered something to them and turned to face me.

"I've fucked around with you too long. I can see they've trained you well. It's time to get serious because you're going to tell me everything I need to know."

I was shaking my head, crying even harder and I knew the interrogation was about to get worse. I could tell by the look on the sergeant's face, the way his two henchmen removed their jackets and rolled up their sleeves. If their actions were meant to terrify me then it had the desired effect. The younger of the two soldiers started on me first, grabbing a handful of my hair and forcing my face flat onto the table. His boss asked the same questions he had asked from the outset. I gave the same answers and each time the soldier banged my head off the wooden table.

After the third or fourth question the side of my face was numb and to be honest the pain didn't register. I think they sensed that and the boss said something to the other soldier.

"Are you thirsty?" he asked.

"Yes," I replied, "yes please, could I have some water?"

I felt so dehydrated, so tired and yet I sensed this was just the beginning. They had no intention of letting me pass out through dehydration. They wanted me to stay conscious. The soldier returned after some minutes. He was carrying a large plastic bottle of water, the condensation on the bottle told me it was ice cold and I licked my lips in anticipation that my thirst was about to be quenched. The soldier walked behind me and then the sergeant stood and appeared to stand to one side. The soldier poured the entire ice-cold contents of the bottle over my head as I gasped in shock struggling to control my breathing.

They were all laughing. They thought it was a great joke that they had fooled me into thinking I would be drinking the water.

The sergeant spoke to his soldier.

"Another one quickly."

The soldier disappeared through the door again and before long had returned with a refill. The boss pushed his seat up to the table and once again the questions started.

"You are good, I'll give you that. You've given me the same answers every time."

I wiped the water from my eyes and as my body temperature dropped and I started to shiver I spoke through the tears.

"They are the same answers because I am telling you the truth."

"Who are you working for, who is your boss?"

"I have no boss, I am not working for anybody."

They poured at least six bottles of water over me until my whole body tingled. At one point I remember my body burning with pain that didn't seem to make sense. I longed for a towel, for a change of dry clothes, to sit in front of a hot fire and thaw out. It was the coldest I could ever remember feeling and at that point would have lied through my teeth if I thought I could have given them the answers they wanted to hear. I just wanted to see my parents' faces again.

After the water treatment, they continued with more violence, the second soldier taking great pleasure in kicking and punching me around the room while the other two looked on laughing. The sadistic bastards were enjoying every minute. How could they treat a human being, a young girl in that way?

I was at the point of passing out as I tucked myself in a ball and curled up in the corner of the room trying to protect my head and face from the soldier's boot but still, the questions continued. I couldn't physically speak, I was so cold. I could feel my body closing down and I longed to die.

I remember praying, wishing that my heart would give out and then it would all be over. I could sleep forever, I would be at peace and I would at last be reunited with my dear cousin and Uncle Demir. The men in uniform would hurt me no more.

I think I must have passed out for some minutes, as there seemed to be a lull in proceedings. I remember thinking that I hadn't been kicked for a while and I dared to turn around to see what was happening. The soldiers were standing over by the table and they were removing something from a box.

"Ahhh... the Muslim whore is with us once again."

The sergeant instructed the two soldiers to strip me and they couldn't wait to comply with his wishes as they almost fell over themselves to get to me. I offered no resistance, I knew it was futile; their horrible slimy palms invaded every inch of my body. I felt humiliated, degraded, dirty and vulnerable but I was more concerned with what the sergeant was doing with the contraption he was holding in his hands. He had walked over to the wall opposite the door and plugged the device into the electric socket.

"This is your last chance to tell me the truth," he said. "Do you know what this is?"

I couldn't speak but was conscious of shaking my head. By now the end of the device was glowing red.

"This building used to be a cattle shed as you can probably tell."

He held it up as he fixed his eyes on it.

"They branded the cattle with one of these. It meant no one could steal their cattle, each brand identified a particular farm."

He gestured to the two soldiers who lunged at me and started to drag me over towards him.

"The cows and the bulls have a thick leathery hide as you know. Sadly human skin is far more delicate and of course, our pain receptors are that much more sensitive."

I bucked and kicked out at the two soldiers as they dragged me ever closer while the sergeant stood in silence. I could see by the look in his eyes that he was enjoying every second as I screamed and pleaded for mercy.

"I gave you every chance but you held out."

"Please…" I begged. "I am telling the truth, I was kidnapped by Kupi, he accused me of spying for Serbia."

The end of the branding iron had turned to a reddish-white colour and I couldn't take my eyes off it. I sensed that the interrogation was over and that sheer torture was about to begin. As with Kupi, I felt that my abusers knew I was telling the truth but it was almost as if that was secondary, not really so important. An unpleasant thought drifted into my head. If they admitted I was telling the truth then they would need to return me back home. There would be an admission that they had been wrong and of course, there wouldn't be any fun for them. It was a frightening thought as my torturer turned to face me.

He spat on the end of the iron and his spit fizzed and bubbled up and was gone in a split second.

"Do you know the difference between pain and acute pain?"

"Please no, I'm telling the truth, I swear on my parents' life."

"Normal pain is a response to an injury, a kind of safety system to tell the brain something is wrong."

The two soldiers had turned me on my stomach, the heaviest one sat on my back. I couldn't see my tormentor now, I could only hear him.

"For example, if you hit your thumb with a hammer it will register pain and therefore the brain will receive a pain signal and it will respond accordingly by telling you not to hit your thumb with the hammer again because if you do you will feel more pain."

His voice was louder now and I assumed he had crouched down behind me.

"Isn't the human brain so clever?"

I heard one of the soldiers giggle.

"But acute pain is very different because acute pain occurs when the injury is more severe and the body is significantly damaged and acute pain lasts until the injury is completely healed."

I felt a hand pull at my hair, my head jerked up and I was staring into his eyes, the branding iron a few centimetres from my face so that I could feel the heat from it.

"The beauty about this contraption is that just a few seconds on the skin can cause several days of acute pain and discomfort."

He slapped me gently on the face in a patronising way.

"Don't worry I won't burn your face," he grinned. "Such a pretty little face."

He stood and walked behind me and I knew he wasn't just threatening me. I felt his hand wrap around the shinbone of my right leg. I tried to kick out but his strong hand and the dead weight on my back rendered it useless.

"I'll ask you one more time, who is your boss?"

"Please," I gasped, barely able to mouth the words, "I'm telling the truth... please believe me."

I heard a deep sigh.

The second soldier reached for my hands and pulled my arms tight as he tensed up and gritted his teeth. He was looking over my shoulder at his sergeant and I could see by the look on his face that the branding iron was dangerously close.

"This is your last chance, Muslim girl."

I barely got the words out between the tears.

"I'm telling the truth," I sobbed, "please... I'm telling you the truth."

"Liar!"

He took a deep breath and pushed the red hot branding iron into the flesh of my left calf and it sizzled like a piece of cooking meat in a pan. At first, I felt the pressure and then the pain kicked in a split second later. It was like nothing I had ever experienced before and I screamed so loud that someone forced their hand over my mouth. It was hard to describe the searing, burning, white-hot feeling, as if my flesh was melting like candle wax but mercifully it didn't last long. I remember the awful smell of burning and then my world started to spin out of control. I knew I was heading for darkness and I prayed to God that my heart had at last given up on me.

CHAPTER EIGHTEEN
THE START OF A NEW NIGHTMARE

It was the pain that woke me. The sergeant's lecture on acute pain had come prophetically true as I slid my hand down towards the burning flesh on my calf. I realised at that point that I had been dressed and I was aware that the material of my jeans was sticking to the raw flesh underneath. I knew I had to pull the denim from the wound and hoped it was still fresh and hadn't healed too much. Mercifully my clothes were still damp from the soaking I'd had and therefore the material a little pliable. I clenched my teeth and pulled gently. The pain was excruciating as millimetre by millimetre I eased the cloth from the bare wound, as it seemed reluctant to give way. Afterwards, I rolled up my trouser leg to my knee to ensure I wouldn't have to go through the process again.

I lay back and tried to focus for a moment. I was lying on some sort of blanket, on a hard stone or concrete floor and it was pitch black. Where was I?

My leg was throbbing so much, pulsing as if it had a heartbeat of its own and there was more pain as I tried to concentrate on the different parts of my body that were now sending signals to my brain and the receptors in my brain were responding and telling me I was in a bad way. I coughed and another pain shot through my lower rib cage then I felt my swollen lips and nose which seemed twice its normal size.

I had experienced this feeling once before but this was different because now I was beyond caring. With Kupi and his gang, I was always thinking of escape, always determined to beat them and in the end I succeeded. Every day with Kupi and his gang had been torture related either mentally or physically, sometimes both, but I had tried to remain positive as the weeks passed by. I couldn't go through that all over again, I knew I would never make it, I didn't have the strength or the courage. I had used up every bit of resolve within me. I had nothing left, a day or two at the most and as much as I didn't want to admit it, the Serbian Army or whoever it was who had captured me would break my spirit far sooner than they could ever have imagined.

I lay in the same position for some time and the tears rolled freely down my cheeks and I even recall being annoyed that my body was reacting in that way. I kept wiping the tears with my sleeve and after a while, they'd subside and then I'd recall that only a few short hours ago I'd been reunited with my darling parents and then it had all gone horribly wrong and I'd feel sorry for myself and the tears would start all over again.

I could make out the shape of the room. It was so very small and I could just about make out the form of a door as the faint chink of light shined through the cracks at either side. I cautiously stretched out my injured leg taking care that it didn't touch the face of the woollen blanket. Before I could extend my leg fully it came into contact with a wall. I reached behind me into the darkness and my hand immediately touched the surface of the other wall. My God! The room was smaller than the length of my body. I began to panic. This wasn't a room. It wasn't even big enough to be a standard prison cell. Was it a tomb? Had I been buried alive? I jumped up quickly and reached for the ceiling. It was no more than three centimetres above my head. I breathed a sigh of relief. At least I could stand. But my cell was tiny, not much bigger than a small broom cupboard. Surely they couldn't keep me in here too long?

I paced my cell out, three steps long by two paces wide and just enough height to stand and accommodate my one hundred and seventy centimetres frame. I ran towards the door screaming, banging on the door demanding to be let out. The claustrophobia was worse than any torture, worse than any beating I had experienced.

I hammered on the door until my hands felt like pieces of frozen meat until I could feel them no more and eventually I collapsed in a heap onto the blanket. I tried to listen between the tears but no one came. I listened for hours, listened for the sound of voices, of vibrations, perhaps a door closing in a distant part of the building but I heard nothing, it was as quiet as an empty Mosque.

I lost all track of time as I cried for what seemed like hours but eventually, the panic subsided and I lay in a semi-comatose state. I figured I was in some sort of cupboard with a reinforced steel door and I could now make out the shape of a boarded-up grill in the door. I slept. I cried. I slept and cried and every now and again I banged on the door but still no one came.

It's impossible to gauge time when you have no watch and there is no natural light. The day-time becomes night-time because it is always dark. As much as I studied the walls and looked to see if there was any change in the light pattern they always looked the same. I started to count to sixty then one hundred and twenty, then one hundred and eighty, mentally ticking   off the minutes in my head, calculating an hour, and then counting those hours on the fingers of my hand. As hard as I tried I couldn't count more than three hours before I fell to sleep.

Each time I awoke the blanket had stuck to my calf and I endured the agony of tearing my damaged flesh from the coarse wool. In the end, I took to sleeping on my stomach, which seemed to work and eventually, the wound dried. It was still painful to the touch, but bearable. I guessed from the condition of my wound that I had been there at least two days and still no one appeared.

I dreamt that someone had entered my tomb. When I awoke the cell was filled with a beautiful aroma and as I made my way towards the door on my hands and knees I reached out cautiously, as I followed my nose and found a bowl of hot soup, a chunk of bread and a bottle of water. I devoured it instantly. The soup was delicious, vegetable of some sort but quite the tastiest soup I had ever had. I realised just how hungry I was as I mopped it up with the dry bread. I even licked the bowl I was so hungry and dehydrated. Afterwards, I drained every drop of the water from the bottle. It took no more than a minute and almost immediately I realised how silly that was. My belly was now full but uncomfortably so. I'd gorged myself without even thinking.

I hadn't heard or seen anyone come into my cell. When would they be back?

Several hours later I got the urge to pee. I walked over to the door and started to bang. There was a small grill just above head height that had been blocked with a piece of wood and four vertical iron bars. I eased myself up by holding two of the bars and shouted for help through the crack in the wood. I didn't expect to get an answer but within a minute I heard two voices on the other side of the door.

"What do you want mother fucker?"

It felt so good to hear human voices again even though I knew how menacing they were.

"The toilet. I need to go to the toilet please."

"There's a toilet in there."

"No there's not," I replied.

"Yes there is, there's one in every corner."

I heard the sound of the two men laughing and then the sound of their boots walking away on the stone floor. Eventually, the sound faded into the distance.

They were right, there was a toilet in every corner so I chose the corner nearest to the door, undid my jeans and peed. I was conscious that my urine ran out from under the gap in the door and outside into the room where the guard's voices had come from. They would have to clean it up. Perhaps next time they would listen to me.

Within a few days, I realised that the food wasn't so delicious, it was just that I had been so hungry. They brought me something generally twice a day, mostly the same sort of soup. It contained vegetables, usually carrots and potatoes with slices of onions and occasionally it smelled a little like chicken. The first time I smelled the soup I got quite excited and raked through it for the meat but found nothing. For several days I searched for that meat but then gave up realising that it was only the flavour of the powdered stock and not made from any real chicken after all.

Sometimes they brought me bread and butter for breakfast, occasionally there would be a sachet of strawberry jam and that would be all they'd give me until suppertime when the soup would be brought into my cell again. They also brought me a bean broth, a chicken flavoured soup filled with beans. My bean broth broke up the monotony of the other soup and I looked forward to it.

But my food pattern was very irregular, some days they seemed to forget about me altogether, and I remember on one occasion going for two or three days without anything at all. The hunger pains were unbearable.

I think the soldiers had been called away somewhere because during these days there was no sound of any kind anywhere in the building. I dragged my blanket over to the door and sat for hours trying to hear some sort of noise. All I heard was the wind and the rain outside. I convinced myself they had abandoned the building and I would slowly starve to death. That suited me fine, I wanted to die but I confess I was a little frightened thinking what starving to death would be like. I knew it would be a slow, painful process and I began to think of ways I could tear my blanket up into strips and hang myself. That would surely be a better way to go.

CHAPTER NINETEEN
RATS, MICE AND COCKROACHES
AND THE MOST EVIL ANIMALS
ON THE PLANET

It didn't take me long to figure out night and day. I remember being terrified at first as I heard the scuttling of the cockroaches on the far side of the cell but told myself as long as I heard them on the stone floor it meant they weren't anywhere near my blanket. I remembered at school one day when my teacher set an exercise on nocturnal animals and insects and she told us that cockroaches were very much nocturnal creatures. Although I didn't particularly like cockroaches I wasn't petrified of insects in the same way some of my old friends from school were. I could handle the noises of the cockroaches easily enough. Rats and mice however were a different matter. They were my worst nightmare!

So I started listening for the cockroaches, which was a kind of cue to try and go to sleep. This meant I could control my body clock once again and in a way it was strangely comforting that I could at least control something. I assumed because I would be awake during the day that I would be able to see who brought my food and water and I would be able to strike up a conversation with the guards asking them how long I would be there and when I would be going home. But this wasn't always the case, the food was nearly always delivered while I was sleeping.

After several days I really needed to go to the toilet and fought sleep late into the night until they brought in my food. I pleaded with the guards not to make me mess in my cell. Eventually, they gave in and opened the door. One of the guards was dark with short hair and a stubbly unkempt beard. He had dark, almost Middle Eastern features, slightly overweight with a small button nose. His colleague was altogether much thinner with fair skin, they looked almost comical standing together. They both wore army uniforms and white training shoes.

I walked through, into the large room. I remember feeling so happy that it was light and at last, I'd seen something different. I recall even smiling but my joy was short-lived. The guards pointed to a small cubicle over the far side of the room and then told me that I was a "demanding bitch" and that they would beat me to the toilet and all the way back again.

And they did. Before I could protest I was aware of a flailing arm flying through the air but I managed to duck just in time as it bounced fairly harmlessly off my shoulder. I then felt the sole of a boot in the small of my back and a slap across the head as I turned tail and ran as fast as I could towards the toilet. They chased after me laughing and squealing like two small children taking great delight in every blow they landed. It was all a game to them but I made it in one piece and bolted the door behind me. I sat on the toilet looking around. To my disappointment there were no other exits, no windows but to my relief there was toilet paper and a sink with some soap. I took my time and washed and thankfully the soldiers didn't seem to mind how long I was in there. They knew I wasn't going anywhere and I listened to their conversation as they talked about some sort of football tournament that was taking place on the other side of the world.

When I came out they kicked and punched me all the way back to the cell but I ran fast and dodged most of the blows and congratulated myself on a small victory when I made it back and they closed the door behind me. I sat on my blanket breathing hard and for the first time in a long time, felt small beads of perspiration on my brow and yet I felt clean. In a perverse sort of way, that's all that seemed to matter to me.

One of the soldiers shouted through the grill in the door.

"Just so you know you Muslim bitch, that's what happens every time you come out of there."

I turned towards the door in the blackness, my knees raised to my chin and I wondered if my eventful expedition to the toilet had been worth it.

That was short-lived as they came back, opened my door with so much force, grabbed me by the feet and dragged me towards them. One pulled my trousers off while the other pinned me down and closed my mouth with his filthy hand. The other one took his trousers down controlling my legs as he lay on top of me. He raped me. The pain was excruciating. I was crying and struggling to breathe. Soon they swapped places, and the other raped me too. I instantly felt sick, and I just wished they would kill me while they violated me, as they had taken my innocence forever.

Once they were done, they stood up, spat on me and walked away slamming my prison door behind them. I cried and screamed with all the energy I had left in me, lying there in disgust like a statue, letting the darkness of the room and the darkness of my mind take me away. There and then I knew that I was never going to be the same again. Depression took over, I was suicidal. If only I could take my own life. I prayed to the darkness to show me the way to end this torment. "

If there is a God, why is this happening to me? Please, my deepest disturbing darkness, show me the way." I pleaded.

To my surprise, my mind's coping mechanism kicked in. I began to experience amazing colours in the darkness. I could stare into the corner of my cell and see almost an explosion of shades of reds and yellows and bright purples. At times it seemed like the whole cell was on fire. The flames and spirals and lightning bolts and flashes mixed together and changed colour blending into each other. The purples turned to green then silver and gold and then bright, bright white and eventually back to purple again. It was like my own personal firework display, a huge kaleidoscope and if I concentrated really hard they were still there when I closed my eyes. The colours in the darkness were somehow comforting to me and I perfected the art so that they would come to me in seconds rather than the hour or two I'd had to stare into the blackness when it happened for the first time. Sometimes I would recall a classical piece of music and put the two together and it was so peaceful as I closed down my entire mind to the horrors around me. This was what it must be like to be on hallucinogenic drugs I thought to myself. Who needs drugs when you have the powers of the mind?

I was back out in the main room a few days later having taken the decision to chance another beating or being sexually abused. I only needed to pee and it would have been far easier to go in my cell but I was aware that I was growing more and more depressed sitting alone in the darkness and knew that even a few minutes of viewing the change in surroundings always lifted my spirits a little even though it meant the chance of an attack at the hands of my two sadistic guards.

I had my plan ready. This time I would bolt out as soon as there was enough space but immediately drop to my hands and knees to try and take them by surprise. It worked well as I fooled them completely and they fell over themselves trying to reach me. I made it to the toilet very easily and even allowed myself a casual look back over my shoulder to watch them sprawling all over the floor as they cursed and bickered with each other, each one blaming the other for their inability to catch me.

My joy was short-lived. I turned on the light in the toilet and made my way over to the cubicle. The small brown field mouse was probably more shocked and more frightened than I was as it shot out from under the cubicle door in my direction. I shrieked at the top of my voice as I nearly took the toilet door from its hinges and shot past the startled guards before they had a chance to lay a hand on me. I heard them laughing as they no doubt spotted what it was that had given me such a fright. I was back in my cell quicker than I had managed before and slammed the door behind me. The guards came over to my cell taunting me that they had caught the little mouse and would be keeping it for a little fun at a later date.

Although I had avoided another sexual assault, I didn't sleep at all that night. Convinced that the two evil creatures on the other side of the door would release the mouse into my cell as I slept, or worse.

CHAPTER TWENTY
TO DIE OR NOT TO DIE;
THAT IS THE QUESTION

As the weeks turned into months, I'd lie on my blanket for hours hoping they'd come to get me and take me somewhere. I didn't care where. They could come to execute me, rape me, they could come to question and interrogate me. I didn't mind. Anything was better than the darkness and sheer boredom. I couldn't say at that point that I felt any fear, only the fear of the unknown and because I was never told what was going to happen it was impossible to feel real fear. Kupi was different. He had terrified me because Kupi told me everything that was going to happen to me and it was like something from a horror movie.

The cell was freezing, we were in the mountains somewhere, I knew that and although it was springtime I knew how cold spring could be outside of the towns and villages. The cell was draughty, the wind whistled through the dilapidated farm building and cut under my cell door causing a vacuum and at times my teeth chattered for so long I'd convince myself that even if I did get out I'd do my teeth permanent damage. At times, generally in the early hours of the morning, the cold would wake me and it was nigh on impossible to get back to sleep.

Apart from the cold, the boredom was the worst. The only thing to keep my mind occupied was my own imagination. The little decisions became the biggest part of my mind's occupation. When the food and bread and water came I'd take an age to decide what went down my throat first. Some days it was the water, other days it was the soup, especially if it was warm. That would be a real treat. Some days I'd test myself to see how much dried bread I could eat before washing it down with the water, or the soup. Everything became a game and I wondered at what point I would start to lose my mind. Surely being kept in solitary confinement in constant darkness would make it only a matter of time?

Going to the toilet in the corner of my cell or running the gauntlet of fists and boots became another big daily decision and I learned to somehow limit my bowel movements. Most days I decided to pee in the cell, sometimes I felt brave and in need of a little exercise so I took them on. The punches, the kicks and the sexual assaults no longer hurt. They couldn't possibly hurt me because there comes a time when you have been abused so many times it stops hurting. Parts of my face were almost numb, certainly my cheekbones and my lips, they were almost permanently swollen. I counted my blessings convincing myself that my swollen lips would at least protect my teeth.

I'd listen at the door for the guards entering the room and I'd psyche myself up until the adrenalin was pumping around my body. The conversation was always the same... short.

I'd bang on the door.

"I need to go to the toilet," I'd shout.

"Are you sure?"

It was the fair-skinned soldier. He had a high-pitched squeaky voice and at times he sounded like an old woman.

"Yes."

"You know what that means?"

"Yes."

One of them would walk forward and unlock the door and they'd stand back to let me run out. It was a game for them and a game for me. I'd wait a few minutes in the hope I'd catch them off guard and I'd sprint out and either turn quickly to my left or my right depending on where they stood, desperately trying to avoid the initial onslaught. Sometimes they'd miss me and it was an all-out sprint to get to the toilet first. Because of the condition I was in I'd invariably get hit or tripped before I reached the safety of the toilet door but now and again I'd make it without getting touched. They'd allow me up to fifteen minutes and I'd enjoy every delicious, peaceful second as I stripped off and washed but knew it would begin again as soon as I left the sanctity of the small W.C. It was all rather sad. They were playing mind games with me and it was taking its toll.

To be or not to be, that is the question. It was a quote from Hamlet and it came to me in the middle of the night as I listened to the cockroaches in the corner of my cell. I remembered studying Hamlet at school, remembered my teacher analysing the quote and discussing what it was all about. Hamlet was musing about the conundrum of suicide. It was a poignant subject to be thinking about in my present predicament. Hamlet wondered if it was a noble way out. He was unable to act upon his motives for revenge and it frustrated him. Was it better to suffer or better to end it all? Hamlet related his personal struggle to the struggles that all men suffer from at some point in their lives. But Hamlet didn't know what happened after death so therefore realised that death wouldn't be the ideal escape he craved.

* * *

The guards burst into my cell one morning and announced it was wash time. They told me they had noticed that I had begun to smell and were more than aware that my clothes hadn't been near a washing machine for many weeks. They ordered me out into the main room and told me to strip and throw my clothes into a plastic bin which they said would be incinerated. I had no choice but to comply. I stripped down to my bra and knickers.

One of them stepped forward.

"Everything."

He pulled out a flick knife and snapped it open, slicing the strap of my bra with the razor-sharp blade.

"Next time it will be your fucking face, now do as you're told."

I had no choice but to remove my underwear and tried to conceal my modesty with my hands, as I stood stark naked in front of the two guards who by now couldn't take their eyes off me. They ordered me to start walking and pointed me in the direction of another door about twenty metres from the toilet. It was locked and one of them opened it with a key. We walked through the door and down a short corridor to another one, which he also unlocked. I took note of everything around me and couldn't help noticing that there were no windows anywhere. There were no windows in my cell or the large room it opened onto, nor were there any windows in the toilet and no windows in the corridors either. But why would there be? It was a farm and cows and sheep didn't need windows.

We walked about thirty metres and the corridor turned sharply to the left. There was a white tiled area with what looked like a series of showerheads. I supposed this was where they cleaned the animals prior to a market sale or another purchase. Did they even wash animals? I didn't know.

They told me to step forward and stand under one of the shower taps. One of the guards walked back around the corner and within a few seconds, water started to pour out. It was icy cold and my immediate reaction was to jump to the side to get out of the way. The guard slapped my backside hard and forced me back under the water but to my amazement, the water gradually started to heat up. It was so good, the warmest I had been in a long while and for a brief moment I forgot the guards were even there.

They soon made their presence felt. I noticed one of them had taken off his jacket and rolled up his sleeves. He had a bar of soap in his hands and he ordered me forward. I did as I was told. As his colleague stood by grinning he soaped my body all over paying special attention to my breasts. He was clearly enjoying himself and I knew what was coming. I'd fought against Kupi's gang when they were going to rape me but I had already conceded defeat in here. As much as I hated to admit it there was no fight left in me.

After five minutes or so he was finished and pushed me back under the shower and I rinsed the soap away. I was ordered out again and this time it was the other guard's turn to have his fun. Bizarrely he spent more time washing my hair than any other part of my body and I'm ashamed to say I enjoyed it because I was clean and warm.

They then dried me gently with clean towels. I felt as if I was going crazy. Were these the same men who beat me every time I needed to leave my cell to go to the toilet? I even wondered if I had imagined those beatings, if they had been bad nightmares. They walked me back towards the cell. I expected a sting in the tail, a beating or worse. Outside the cell door was a pile of clean clothes, socks, a pair of very large panties, a t-shirt, a jumper and some jeans and they ordered me to dress. The clothes smelled fresh, they were even a little warm and I guessed they'd been freshly laundered. When I had dressed they turned me around and inspected me much like a soldier on parade. When they were happy they pushed me back in the cell and locked the door. As incredible as it may seem I felt happy and I felt strong and clean.

My shower days were a mind fuck. On one side I looked forward to getting cleaned up and having a bigger space to escape the claustrophobia of my grave-like cell and enjoy the calming effect that the water had on my skin, but on the other side I was petrified of the mental, physical, and sexual abuse. At first, the showers happened every few days, then perhaps once a week but eventually they were very irregular indeed. I guess it was whenever the guards decided to have their fun.

One day I made the mistake of requesting the toilet on the way back from the shower. I was clean and warm and dressed but off guard, as I walked into the W.C. I did what I had to do and walked back out never suspecting that they were going to start. The guard who had caressed and washed my hair just a few minutes earlier punched me hard in the stomach and I collapsed in a heap on the floor. I had the presence of mind to know what was happening and scuttled quickly between his legs as the other one aimed kicks at me. I was up on my feet and sprinting towards the door but I was too slow as one of them gripped my hair and hauled me backwards. I crashed onto the floor and curled up in a ball in a vain attempt to shield myself from the kicks and slaps and punches that rained down on me. They beat me until they were out of breath, they kicked me until I lapsed into unconsciousness and I awoke to find I was back in the cell once again. I ached all over. I had never been beaten like that for some time. They had certainly won the battle that day and I learned a valuable lesson to never to trust them again.

I would lie awake trying to figure out what made these men tick. I suspected they were bored too but couldn't work out how they could be so gentle one minute and so vicious the next. They were sadists, of that there was no doubt, unpredictable, possibly even schizophrenic, though what were the chances of two guards on the same duty being that way? No, these men were not ill, they were just men in a conflict and as I'd discovered with the Kupi gang, when there is conflict and war, all reasoning is pushed to the furthest recesses of the human brain, as if someone grants a special licence to turn men into twisted, multi-personality monsters.

I would lie awake and daydream. I'd imagine I was a small girl again and dream of the good times I'd had, the walks in the mountains with my parents, the grand feasts and family reunions at Uncle Demir's and the family holidays we'd spent on the beach at Montenegro called Ulcinj. I worked hard at daydreaming and I'd work hard at the colours in the darkness because it transported me away from the nightmare I was in and I became quite good at them both.

For hours and hours, I would be lost in another world, my own, personal moving picture with my good friends from my childhood as the co-stars. My cell didn't exist, the beasts outside my cell door forgotten about, the beatings, the rape and abuse a distant memory, as I'd take myself down memory lane. I'd walk back and forward in my cell with my eyes closed, one two three steps turn… one two three and I'd take myself back to the past. I was no longer in that cell I was on a beach, a mountainside, driving a car or just sitting at the kitchen table with my beautiful parents. We'd be eating Sarma or Suxhuk, a delicious Turkish-style sausage or pite, a meat and potato pastry pie and of course, I would always finish with baklava, my favourite dessert. Sometimes I'd sing to myself or recite a poem I'd been taught at school. It was quite incredible the power of recall and the more I remembered the more I convinced myself that perhaps I wasn't losing my mind after all.

I studied Romeo and Juliet and I studied my favourite quotes, quotes that I'd read over and over again as a teenager so that they were lodged deep in my brain, so deep that no one could ever take them away from me and despite the fact I had no books I could still study. One quote came to me over and over again and it somehow gave me comfort during my darkest hours of despair.

Her blood is settled, and her joints are stiff; Life and these lips have long been separated: Death lies on her like an untimely frost. Upon the sweetest flower of all the field.

I loved my Nani and Agi, they were my superheroes, they made me what I was, and at times when I wanted to give up I'd think of them. I'd dare to believe that they may just have survived and I owed it to them to fight through the torment. So I'd get up and start my walk again, one, two, three, one, two, three and I'd fill my head with the images of their faces from happier times and I'd be alive again, cocooned in my own, perfect world.

But all too often my daydreams would be ripped apart, reality would come crashing through the cell door as regularly as clockwork. I hadn't been showered for some time. I didn't know how long because one day, one week, one month merely blended into another.

I recollect one particular day, perhaps three months into my captivity, when one of the guards brought the food in and stood at the door with a strange look on his face. The only light that reached me was when the cell door was opened, otherwise, I was always alone in the cell in the darkness. I could only see his silhouette at first but then the features of his face came into focus.

"What wrong?" I asked.

"You fucking stink, that's what's wrong." He said.

And almost immediately I knew what it was that smelt. I hadn't had a period for some months but a few nights back I'd awoken with familiar feeling stomach cramps. I thought nothing of it. The next morning I thought I'd felt a dampness between my legs but put it down to urine. My bladder control was weak, due to the fact my body clock was all over the place and my internal organs battered and bruised because of the numerous beatings at the hands of the brothers Grimm. There were many occasions that I'd ended up lying in my own urine or faeces before I'd managed to make it to the sanctuary of the toilet.

"Over here you dirty bitch. Let me take a look at you."

I shuffled over to the door and he pulled me into the light by my hair. I looked down between my legs. My jeans were stained a reddish brown colour and immediately we both knew what had happened. I was mortified, so ashamed, so embarrassed that a stranger had witnessed me this way.

The guard was furious as he screamed for his friend.

"You filthy bitch," he spat.

As if I could help it.

"If you can get me some towels or tissue paper it won't happen again."

"Take your clothes off," he barked.

The soldier rived at my jumper and blouse and then tore my bra from me throwing it to the ground. He graciously allowed me to remove my soiled jeans and knickers myself and pushed me against the outside wall of the cell.

His colleague arrived and he told him to prepare the shower and some clean clothes. He made me stand naked for some time until his friend returned and they frogmarched me to the showers. I felt dirty and looked forward to the warm shower and the sweet-smelling soap, it had been a long time and a change of clothes would be welcome too.

I was to be sorely disappointed as they pushed me into the corner and produced what looked like a powerful length of hose. They connected it up to a large tap that stood a metre from the floor and turned it on. The powerful jet hit me in the chest and knocked me over onto the shiny tiled floor. The water was freezing-cold at first but as with the showers, I expected the hot water would soon kick in. I wasn't to be so lucky this time as the hose was only connected to a cold water outlet.

They laughed and giggled and squealed like tormented schoolboys as they tried their hardest to hose the flesh from my bones. At first, the jet of cold water was painful and stinging but within minutes my whole body was numb with the cold and I felt no pain. They aimed the powerful jet at my head and the force of it cracked my cheekbone into the tiles. I could do nothing but crawl into a corner and curl up in a ball with my back to them. They swore and cursed at me and it became like a language of its own, every other word a foul-mouthed expletive, and whilst at first it bothered and hurt me, I was beyond caring and expected no better from these animals. The hose stopped and I felt two hands grab me roughly as they turned me around and pulled me into the centre of the tiled area. One of them prised my legs apart and then they turned the hose on and aimed the cold jet between my thighs. Although I had my eyes closed I sensed one of the guards was quite close to me. He was telling his colleague how much I was enjoying the experience. Although I was living in fear every day of being sexually abused and this monstrous act never got easier, I somehow believed that during my monthly cycle, they wouldn't be interested. I was wrong. As they raped me, I couldn't hold back the tears and screams of fear and agony. Once they were done, I made it back into the corner and curled up in a ball while they laughed and giggled.

It's hard to tell how long I was abused in the shower unit, probably no more than ten minutes but it was ten minutes that lasted an eternity. All the while they taunted me calling me the vilest, filthiest names they could dream up. Eventually, they turned off the hose and lifted me to my feet. I tried to stand unaided but the signals transmitted from my brain to my lower limbs went unanswered and if they hadn't held on to me I would have collapsed in a heap. My teeth chattered and banged together which was a great source of amusement to them as they made comments about how a woman could never keep her mouth closed.

I don't know how I managed to walk back to the cell as my feet felt like two blocks of ice. They threw me back into my cell with a towel and my clean clothes. As I slowly began to thaw out my whole body seemed to tingle and burn and both hands were fixed like claws which meant I couldn't even hold the towel let alone dress myself. Thankfully it was summer now and the cell wasn't particularly cold. If it had been winter or even early spring, I wouldn't have survived the night. The pain was excruciating, my whole body cried out for release and my head ached like it had never ached before, like someone had squeezed a big bass drum in there, pounding away as if their life depended on it. The headache was the worst, relentless; I thought it would never end. I remembered my father telling me that if I was in pain to squeeze hard on a pressure point between my thumb and my forefinger. I tried the process for several minutes but it didn't take the pain away.

It was many hours before I was able to dress fully and the pain in my head eventually subsided. I wrapped myself up in the blanket and tried to fall asleep as I heard the cockroaches making their nightly expedition across the stone floor.

CHAPTER TWENTY-ONE
WHY DO THEY NOT COME
FOR ME?

The days and the weeks rolled into one. I knew that I had been in my own personal tomb for many months now. The general change in the temperature of the cell told me that, as it turned from freezing cold to bearable and then week by week gradually started to warm up. As mid-summer took hold, at times it was stiflingly hot in there. And yet I longed for that sun, to see it rising up from a mountainside gradually casting light over the valley. I had forgotten what the sun looked like. I craved the warmth, the way it made you feel when you were able to sunbathe to the point of perspiration and then cool off in the sea or, in a crystal clear blue swimming pool.

But I knew there was no hope of escape and by now I had given up the thoughts of anyone coming to rescue me, of ever seeing the sun again. I was lost in my mind that was by now playing strange hallucinogenic tricks on me and wondered if I could ever find myself again. I fought on and tried to complete everyday tasks that other people would take for granted. My fingernails were like claws and ugly, so I took to sanding them on the concrete floor but left them long enough so that I could scrape in between my teeth. Keeping my teeth clean without a toothbrush was almost impossible but I tried my best with my fingers and my nails. I forget how many times I asked my guards for a toothbrush and toothpaste, period pads and even a hairbrush but nothing ever materialised. It was probably just as well they didn't bring a hairbrush, as by now my tangled, matted hair was falling out in clumps. I'd only have to drag my fingers through my scalp and the hair would come loose in my hands. My scalp was raw and tender, painful to the touch and my skin was dry and flaking off like talcum powder.

I cried myself to sleep many nights as I thought about my parents and because they'd never come to get me I assumed they had been murdered. It was the only logical explanation. Agi would never have allowed me to stay there so long.

I started to bite myself, sometimes as hard as I could and at times managed to puncture the skin and draw blood. It felt good. It felt that at least I was in control of the pain. It was different to the pain and torture my captors inflicted on me because it was my pain not theirs. I bit my fingers and my forearms and even my shoulders and my knees if I pulled them up towards my chin. On one occasion I remember biting my shoulder so hard that I could feel the sensation of the blood trickle all the way down to my hand. I waited and guided the stream of blood, using gravity and felt so pleased as it reached my wrist and then licked the trail all the way back up to my shoulder. I sat in the darkness grinning with blood smeared all over my face. At that point, I knew I was dangerously close to becoming a psychotic, deranged lunatic. I wondered what my captors would have thought if they had walked in on me at that moment.

And yet I had moments of rational normality and lucid thoughts. I asked myself why I had never been questioned or interrogated again, analysing every little detail. It made no sense. If they genuinely thought I was a spy then surely that one day of interrogation was not the first and the last time. And yet the more I thought about it the more it made perfect sense. They would never question me again because they knew the answers would always be the same, they knew I had told the truth, knew I wasn't a spy, just like Kupi and his gang, the truth had no relevance. The only thing I couldn't quite understand was why they were keeping me alive, why were they bringing me food every day?

My mood swings told me that I was heading towards the thin line where sanity ends and madness begins. It was incredible the emotions I went through in such a short time. I became aggressive, ready and willing to attack the guards as they opened my cell door and more than happy to fight the monsters I faced as I ran the almost daily gauntlet to the toilet. I'm ashamed to admit that sometimes I even enjoyed the confrontation.

Occasionally my energy levels seemed to increase for no apparent reason and I'd find myself pacing back and forward in my cell for hours at a time. I was hallucinating too, patterns would appear on the cell walls even though I could hardly see them and sometimes when I closed my eyes I'd see arrangements of stars and bright lights. As always I was paranoid about the rats and the mice coming into my cell. Sometimes I'd wake from a particularly bad nightmare as the vermin poured into my cell and ran all over me. I'd always wake up at the point when the largest, ugliest rat was creeping up my chest to my face so that our noses were just about touching. His whiskers would be twitching and I'd know he was just about to launch himself towards me.

One day that nightmare came true.

I could hear the guards giggling outside the cell door and I knew they were up to something. They shouted that there were friends who had come to visit, and asked if I wanted to see them. I suspected they were lying but they kept on at me and said that they would only allow them into the cell if I sanctioned the visit. One of the guards opened the small grill in the door by sliding the wood to one side.

I could see his face through the bars and he was quoting some provision from the Geneva Convention.

"Every prisoner has the right to a visit but every prisoner also has the right to refuse."

I fell right into their trap.

"But who is it, who has come to visit me?"

"I can't tell you that I'm afraid."

I dared to imagine that my father had somehow survived and had found out where I was. Could it be Brian or Peter, perhaps both of them or was it the lawyer or the solicitor I'd requested so often? Different possibilities and scenarios raced around my head. Had they checked up on my case number and verified my story, was it a policeman or perhaps a UN official?

The guards seemed unusually patient for a change, listening carefully as I asked questions. I knew it was a ridiculous situation because they could have opened the door any time they wanted and yet I began to wonder if they were perhaps telling the truth. It did sound as if the guard was reading from a sheet, perhaps the Geneva Convention stated just that.

"I'll ask you one more time," he said, "do you wish to receive your visitors or not?"

Visitors…more than one. Brian and Peter

"Yes, yes, of course I do. Please open the door, I'll come and see them."

"No need, they'll come to see you."

At that point, one of them laughed and I knew I had been duped. The cell wasn't big enough for me never mind more than one visitor. I took two steps back and almost fell against the far wall as I heard the key being turned in the lock.

No… no… surely not. Not that, anything but that.

They flung the door open and the two of them took a step inside. My eyes grew accustomed to the light and I focussed on a small cage one of the guards held up in front of me.

"Your visitors." He grinned.

I recoiled in horror as I focussed on a writhing mass of rodent bodies, at least half a dozen mice and poking his nose through the bars at the front of the cage was a huge black rat bearing his teeth.

"No please, please, anything, I'll do anything but don't …"

I didn't get time to finish my sentence before he'd knelt down and opened the front of the cage. The small mice scurried out into the darkness and disappeared while the big rat took a single step forward and paused as his whiskers twitched and he analysed the situation. Before I could react the guards had slammed the cell door and locked it leaving me alone with my worst possible nightmare. I could hardly breathe as my lungs lurched into panicking spasms. Instinctively I ran forward and leapt at the door, grabbing the iron bars with my hands and lifting my knees up to the cold metal so that my feet were several centimetres from the floor. And I screamed. I screamed for all I was worth as my fear turned to panic and the tears flowed like they'd never flowed before. How could they do this to me? More importantly, how could they take such pleasure and amusement at the sheer terror they were putting me through?

As weak as I was, as wasted as my muscles were, I held onto that door for dear life and if I'd had to hold on for twenty-four hours then I would have done so. I could hear the creatures scurrying around beneath me and there was nothing worse I could possibly imagine than to set my bare feet on that stone floor and give them access to me, a stepping stone to the rest of my body. I screamed and I pleaded through the bars in the grill but mostly I screamed. In the end, I think they opened the door because they could bear the noise no more. When I was sure that every single mouse and the large rat had run from the cell, I collapsed onto the floor. My arms were on fire, my knees numb and my thigh muscles ached as though someone had pushed a thousand hot needles into each one.

I was at rock bottom, I couldn't stand it, couldn't take this anymore. I wanted to die and that night I asked God to take me yet again, begging him to listen to me and spare my anguish. I had taken the abuse and the punishment, the beatings, the rapes and the threats, but this was one thing I knew I couldn't come back from.

The cockroaches were no longer welcome in my cell because in the darkness I convinced myself that they were mice and rats and I broke out into a cold sweat every time I heard them. I'd sit up in the corner by the door and wrap my blanket around me until I worked it up to my chin so that only my head was visible. And I'd fight the sleep because I had to be alert in order to kick those mice or cockroaches away as soon as they got anywhere near the bottom of my blanket.

The result was that I exhausted myself to the point of no return. I was a living zombie and for many days I didn't even have the energy to crawl over towards the door and take my food. I think the guards realised how close I was to death and thankfully their little joke was never repeated and they urged me to eat. And yet I could never understand that. Surely it was better for me to die? They weren't going to put me on trial and they weren't going to let me go so what was the point in keeping me alive?

Gradually, for some reason I couldn't explain, I began to eat again. One day I tore tiny strips from my blanket, crawled over to where the unassuming cockroaches made their nightly march across the cell floor and blocked up all of the holes. I figured they took off and found another piece of the building to play in and they never bothered me for several days until eventually they ate their way through the wool blanket.

I slept well apart from the occasional nightmare and steadily my energy returned. I tried to reserve most of that energy contemplating how I could commit suicide without suffering too much pain.

CHAPTER TWENTY-TWO
VIOLATED AGAIN!

I noticed a different voice one day and as I lifted myself up to the grill to concentrate, it came to me that there were three people speaking to each other as opposed to the normal two. I tried to listen in to the conversation but they spoke in whispers. For once they wanted the details of their conversations to remain confidential.

The cell door opened soon after and the stranger stood at the door with the normal two guards flanking him. They said nothing and as he took a step forward the other two guards took a step back and one of them locked the door. I somehow knew what was coming and I had no energy to fight it. He knelt down on my blanket and began to grope at my breasts in the darkness.

I wanted to kick and punch him, I wanted to claw his eyes out but I knew it was all over for me. I prayed this was the end, I prayed that after he raped me he would send me to meet my maker. I was finished. I closed my eyes. He didn't exactly tear my clothes from me, there was no need for that as I offered very little resistance. He pulled at my cardigan and then removed my t-shirt underneath. As he removed my bra and groped and fondled me some more, I was aware that he was breathing quite hard and at one point he pushed himself on top of me while he gyrated up and down. He performed this action for some time and then started to undress me from the waist down at the same time removing his shirt and then his trousers. His rough hands pawed at my vagina as his breathing gained pace and he moaned and groaned stopping occasionally to rub between his own legs.

I could make out the white of his teeth and the sweat on his brow and as he moved and bucked ever faster, little drops of spittle and sweat fell onto my face. His breath smelled of cigarettes and I tensed up as he roughly spread my legs and then his horrible claw-like fingers were inside me. I let out a squeal which seemed to excite him as he panted and grunted and groaned ever harder and then he tensed up, cried out in ecstasy and in an instant collapsed on top of me as gradually his breathing began to return to normal.

I was puzzled. He stood and started to dress. He knocked on the cell door and his colleagues opened it up. As the light flooded in I could make out the shape of their pathetic sneering, grinning faces. He made a show of buckling up his trousers in full view of his friends as they looked on.

"Did you do the Muslim bitch?"

"You bet."

I was disgusted by the pleasure they found in sexually abusing someone. The soldier had ejaculated prematurely, way too prematurely, before he'd even entered me and he stood with his chest puffed out as proud as a peacock as his fellow monsters congratulated him. One of them even slapped him on the back as they left the cell and locked the door behind them.

Although I was being sexually abused repeatedly, I had self-trained myself to block out pain, shame, and the degrading act itself! I took no pleasure or comfort from the fact my rapist hadn't been able to carry out the assignment he'd planned to do. I lay there cold and naked for some hours and the disgusting smell of my attacker would not leave me. His breath was on me, his body odour too and something altogether different and as the smells mingled and lingered and enveloped me like a blanket that smothered me I felt my stomach going into spasms. I rushed over to the corner of the cell where I vomited and brought up the contents of my stomach. I stayed there for some time telling myself that the sour stench of my vomit was better than the stink from my attacker, which had now been absorbed into my blankets.

I banged on the cell door pleading to be showered. I didn't care what type of shower, hot, cold, it didn't matter. My pleas went unheard. The soldiers had gone to celebrate with a beer at one of the local bars no doubt he would entertain them with legendary tales of his sexual prowess. Eventually, I dressed as the cold night air began to penetrate my bones. I still couldn't bring myself to lie on my blankets that night. Wrapping myself in them would be like reliving the attack all over again. I sat on the opposite side of the cell to my sleeping section. I didn't even have the energy to pull my shoes on.

I sat there motionless staring into the blackness. I sat there all night. They brought me some bread and jam the following morning.

I was finished. I would never leave the cell alive. My bread and jam remained untouched, the bean broth they brought that evening went cold until the cockroaches came that night and enjoyed the mother of all feasts. I heard them scuttling all over the plate and I wished them no harm and yet I was strangely jealous of them because although we all lived out our existence in a black stinking hole at least they had freedom of movement and could come and go as they pleased.

Although the cockroaches ate most of my food the guards sensed that I wasn't eating again and it strangely concerned them though I couldn't understand why.

"We know you've stopped eating."

I didn't answer.

"You have to eat."

I ignored them, turned around and faced the wall, which didn't go down too well. One of them grabbed me and pulled me out of the cell. I didn't bother to stand. It was then that they noticed I'd messed myself.

"You dirty bitch."

He turned to his colleague.

"Get the shower hose ready."

I didn't have the energy to stand, I didn't have the energy to eat and I didn't have the energy to request a toilet visit anymore. Running their pathetic gauntlet game was out of the question. So I went to the toilet in my bed. I'd given up all hope and I'd even stopped dreaming. I remembered reading somewhere that when we no longer dream we die. That's where I was and there was a bizarre type of relief in the fact that I'd given up.

They stripped me and dragged me along the corridor to the shower block where they hosed me with the cold hose. I felt nothing, no pain, no coldness... nothing. They dried and dressed me. I told them to leave me alone. They lifted me to my feet and ordered me to walk back to my cell but when they stopped supporting me I simply crumpled to the floor. They shouted and barked at me and I told them to let me die. They dragged me back to the main room and sat me at a table and soon after they brought me some hot bean soup. My head flopped onto the table and that made them angry.

"Eat you bitch," one of them screamed.

"Let me die."

But they wouldn't let me die and instead, they forced the plastic spoon into my mouth until the bowl was empty and I cursed them under my breath.

I shouted at them.

"Why won't you let me die, what good am I to you?"

They didn't answer me.

The following day I soiled myself again, the whole cell stank of excrement and urine and they took me through the whole shower process again, dressed me, and force-fed me at the table. I begged them to let me die but they ignored me and threw me back into the cell again. I would beat them like I had beaten Kupi. I wanted to die and it didn't matter what they did to me they were not going to stop me.

CHAPTER TWENTY-THREE
READY TO MEET MY MAKER

The guard with the high-pitched voice opened the grill the following morning. He told me I had been there six months and for once I believed him. It was particularly hot that morning and judging by the temperature I guessed we were in the middle of summer, July or even August. I had been kidnapped, brought in for questioning at the beginning of February.

He brought my food in, announcing it was bean broth. I told him to take it away. I couldn't move, I was paralysed, I was lying on my right side and it felt as if my whole body had somehow welded itself to the ground. I knew I only had days left to live. Surely if the human body wanted to give up then something somewhere, my heart, my brain or some other internal organ would throw in the towel and that would be it. Although I couldn't see the guard I sensed that he was still there, lingering in the cell for some reason. I turned around and tried to lie on my left side to face him and ask him what he wanted. It was sheer agony as my whole body seemed to groan and creak like the hinges on a squeaky old door. I wanted to open my eyes and stare him out but it was impossible because they hadn't opened for some days. I rubbed at them; they were dry and dusty, I couldn't cry even if I'd wanted to.

"What do you want?" I said blindly.

"You must eat."

"I don't want to eat, I want to die. What's the point of eating it will only prolong my agony."

I listened as he took a step forward. My eyes were closed but I was aware that he'd pushed the bowl of broth towards me as I could smell and feel its warmth only centimetres from the end of my nose. I wanted so much to reach out and take it.

"You must eat."

"Take it away."

I felt his hand on mine and then felt the shape of the bowl as he wrapped my bony fingers around it.

"Take it and eat."

He enclosed my other hand around the other side of the bowl and I held it in two hands. It took all my strength as I tried to open my eyes. Tiny bits of matter and puss coated my eyelids and seemed to fight against me but eventually, gradually they eased apart and as I slowly focussed on the bowl and the guard and the light from the exterior room and the guard with the blond hair and the pointy nose. I could see he was kneeling down beside me.

"You have to eat."

I lifted the bowl towards my face and then as I gave him a little grin I upended the contents on   to the stone floor in front of him as I laughed. It was a final act of defiance and I enjoyed it so much.

He jumped up shouting and screaming.

"You dumb bitch I've a good mind to let you die."

He ranted and raged and I knew he so wanted to take a hold of me and give me a good beating but then that would surely finish me off. Instead, he locked the door and left me there as the broth soaked into the stone floor.

Sometime later, I don't know how long, the other guard opened the cell door. His voice was so much deeper than his companion's.

"You have a visitor. Come out."

I immediately tensed up and a wave of panic shot through me. I knew exactly what had happened the last time he had said that.

"Please no." I whimpered. "I don't want any visitors, leave me alone."

"Seriously you have a visitor."

Almost immediately I noticed there was something different about his tone of voice. But it was another trick surely.

"I want to stay here."

"No, you don't, you want to see your visitor, believe me, you want to see him."

A visitor? Him.

But still, I didn't trust him. I remembered the sheer terror of the day, with clarity, the day   I hung from the grill bars until every muscle, every tendon and every sinew cried out in agony but I wouldn't let go for the fear of what lay beneath me.

I crawled away into the far corner of the cell and I heard him sigh with frustration…impatience… and yet his tone was far from aggressive. On another day he would have stormed into the cell and dragged me out by the hair but this time he stood silhouetted in the doorway.

"You have a visitor," he repeated, "do you want to see him or not?"

I sat trembling. He could have, he would have sent the mice in by now I told myself. And his friend, his colleague, was nowhere to be seen and I couldn't hear anyone laughing. I pitched myself forward and placed my hands on the floor in front of me.

"I have a visitor?"

"Yes."

"No mice or rats?"

"No. A visitor for real."

I edged forward towards the door on my hands and knees. I wanted to stand and I gritted my teeth and pushed with all my might, begging the muscles in my calves and thighs to respond but they let me down. The guard was talking to me and he was different and I couldn't understand. I wanted to stand but I couldn't and I think the guard sensed my frustration and he stepped forward to help me. He had never helped me for six months and suddenly I knew, I sensed that something was happening and that perhaps there was a real visitor after all. I dared to hope and it was almost alien to me because hope was something that had deserted me many months ago. He hooked both hands under my arms and heaved me up, not that it would have taken too much effort. I didn't know at the time but I weighed around six stone, about forty kilos.

I managed to hang on to the frame of the cell door as I tried to regulate my breathing. I was so dizzy and the lights of the main room started to spin. I was on the verge of collapse, totally drained and my eyelids were so very heavy. I wiped at the crusty matter on my eyelids. I still wanted to sleep but for the first time in months, I also wanted to fight it. He propped me against the wall and poured some water from a bottle into my mouth. I drank it voraciously.

"Okay, you have a visitor so try to compose yourself."

"Yes, I will."

I knew now that there were no rats or mice. He lifted me bodily and physically turned me towards the right which was unusual because the only direction I'd ever walked or ran was towards the left, to the toilet and to the corridor that led to the showers.

"Where are we going this isn't the way?"

"To see your visitor."

I held on to him as we walked towards a corridor that led from the far side of the room, the opposite end to the toilet. He was dragging me along the corridor. As much as I tried to summon my strength it seemed a hopeless cause and yet with each step I took I seemed to get stronger and my eyes focussed on where we were going. I felt my lungs begin to burn, but burn in a nice way as a pleasant heat seemed to course through my veins. My heart was beating, pumping with vigour, like it had never pumped for months. There was a door at the far end of the corridor that was slightly ajar and I heard voices piercing the quietness of the corridor, voices that obviously came from that room.

And then I heard a voice that was familiar to me.

It will only be for one night I promise.

"Surely to God no," I whispered under my breath, "it can't be, he's dead, he is surely dead."

It's a deal.

The guard pushed the door open with his foot as he brought me in.

"Here she is."

The door swung open in a weird almost supernatural slow motion and there he was sitting at the same table I'd sat at six months ago. It was the room I had been interrogated in, the room where they had branded me. He raised himself to his feet and his face fell as a look of horror crept across his face.

"My god," he said.

"Agi," I blurted out, "what took you so long?"

My father looked as shocked as I did and after six months of not seeing him, not knowing if he was alive or dead, that was the first thing I said to him.

"What took you so long?" I repeated. "Do you know what they have done to me, how long they have kept me?"

My father turned to the guards.

"What the hell have you done to her, I swear to god I don't recognise my own daughter."

Strangely enough, the two guards looked a little embarrassed as my father walked around the table and at one point I thought he was about to attack them. But he didn't, instead, he held me. It felt so good to be in his arms again and although I had a thousand questions for him I simply buried my head in his chest and cried for some time. My Agi, my beautiful, sweet-smelling Agi.

All too soon the moment had passed. I was aware of raised voices and I felt as if I was floating above the action of the room as they discussed something about a deal and my father berated them for the condition I was in. All I could smell was Agi and it was as if we were almost glued together and I never wanted to be apart from him again.

"Just for one night old man, you understand?"

"Yes, for one night."

"So we have a deal?"

"Yes."

"And you have the money with you?"

"Yes?"

"Where is Nani?" I asked.

My father looked at me and switched from the Serbian language to Albanian.

"Stop asking so many questions," he said.

"Hey old man!" the fat guard said. "Speak Serbian so that we can all understand. What did you say to her?"

Dad stroked at my hair and I was aware that huge lumps were coming away in his hands. "I told her that her mother is not good."

"Where is Nani?" I asked again. "She's dead isn't she?"

Dad took off his suit jacket and wrapped it around me. He always wore a suit jacket no matter the weather.

Despite the warmth of the day I was trembling uncontrollably as chemical reactions I could do nothing about exploded deep within me.

Agi spoke in Albanian again.

"Your mother is fine Lurata."

"You promise Agi?"

"I promise loçki."

That word... *loçki*, my father's darling. *My loçki, my beautiful perfect loçki. You know I love you with all my heart* he had once said with such passion and sincerity. It had been so long since I had heard that word and it sounded so good.

"Speak Serbian! I won't tell you again," the sergeant screamed. "One more word of Albanian shit and the deal is off."

A deal? What deal? My father moved back to the table and reached into a rucksack. He pulled out a clear plastic bag and I could see it was full of Dinar, more money than I had ever seen in my life.

"Just one night," the guard said.

"Yes," my father said, "just to be with her mother."

I stood motionless and speechless as his words sank in. My father was paying them to release me for one night. And yet I didn't care because I would see my mother again and the tiny elements of hope in me began to surface and I dared to think that perhaps my father had contacted the police and lawyers and perhaps they could get me released another night and then perhaps two or three and who knows where that would eventually lead to. Yes, I had hope. I had fallen to the bottom, to the pits of the earth but I could feel myself rising again. The two guards looked on, almost salivating as my father counted out tens of thousands of dinar.

Eventually, he finished.

"As agreed."

The guards nodded and scooped the money from the table placing it into a small cardboard box. They smiled, almost apologetically.

My father stood again and turned to me. He spoke in Albanian, almost as a final act of defiance knowing that the deal was sealed and these greedy bastards were in no mood to call the deal off.

"Come loçki," he said, "We're going home."

CHAPTER TWENTY-FOUR
RESCUED AT LAST

I leaned into my father as he led me along the corridor. His guard had dropped now. He was away from the soldiers and the brave face had gone and he was crying like a baby as he realised the sort of condition his daughter was in. He kept asking me what the monsters had done to me. I kept telling him I was fine and that I wanted to see Nani.

"She's alive?" I kept asking.

"Yes."

"You promise?"

I don't know how many times I asked that question, at least a dozen times before we got to the end of the corridor but I asked the question because every time my father answered he smiled and gradually I began to believe him. When dad smiled, I wanted to smile too. It had been that way since childhood but in that dreadfully long corridor, I couldn't manage one tiny smile. It was as if my face had forgotten what a smile was and it was the most frustrating feeling in the world not being able to smile back at my father.

At the end of the corridor was the door they'd first brought me through. It was ajar and Agi pushed it open with his foot as we stepped outside. I cried out in pain as a million nerve endings exploded in my brain.

"What is it loçki?"

I'd fallen to my knees covering my eyes with my hands. The heat from the sun was glorious as it seemed to scorch my skin and soak into my bones. It was a beautiful moment and yet as soon as it had appeared in my peripheral vision it had blinded me and wracked me with pain.

"What is it Lurata?"

My poor father, I'm sure he must have thought I'd been shot the way I fell to the ground clutching my head. I explained that I hadn't seen the sun for six months and he couldn't quite believe it, cursing and swearing, calling them animals and threatening to take his revenge.

He knelt down beside me and little by little I was gradually able to half open my eyes squinting at the scenery around me. It hurt so much but I wanted to see what *outside* looked like again. I guessed it was midday as the sun was high in the sky, almost directly overhead.

There was an explosion of colour as I looked over towards a mountain and studied the shape of the trees and bushes. It was like being able to see for the first time and it took some time for my brain to register any other colours apart from grey and black. For an instant, I was back in my cell and there was only black. Outside the cell, it was painted battleship grey. That had been my entire colour spectrum for six months. Now I could see the green of the trees and the grass and bright reds and oranges of colourful bushes, the yellows of tiny clumps of flowers and of course the beautiful piercing blue of the sky. I still couldn't look directly at the sun but I could feel it, see the powerful golden glow from the corner of my eye.

Agi lifted me up and supported me and I looked into his beautiful chestnut-coloured eyes. They reminded me of the colour of a thoroughbred racehorse glistening with mild perspiration and I stood for some time staring intently at him taking it all in and then as if by magic a smile pulled across my face.

And Agi smiled too.

"Come, we must go," he said.

We walked over to where the car was parked and he was obviously keen to get away as he opened the back door and told me to get in. We drove for some time and I lay in the back. I think I slept most of the way home and didn't really have any idea how long we had been driving. I was half in a dream by the time we pulled up at the house. I still lay on the back seat but my eyes were open and I could hear my mother's voice.

"Where is she?"

Was I dreaming?

"She's dead, Nani is dead," I whispered.

My father was looking in the car window.

"She's not dead loçki. I promised you. Your Nani is here."

"Where is she?"

I had died, I was surely in heaven and I was happy because I could hear my mother's and my father's voices and I was with them both and that was all that mattered.

Father opened the car door.

"Come and see your mother loçki, she is here."

I crawled from the car somehow summoning up an inner strength and at last, I could stand unaided. I held onto the car door but eventually let go as I picked out the shape of my dear mother standing in the garden twenty metres away. I shuffled towards her like an arthritic old woman.

Nani collapsed crying in a heap before I reached her.

"My god what have they done to you?"

"I'm fine Nani, really I am."

I looked up at her and smiled.

"I remembered what you once said Nani, what doesn't kill you makes you stronger."

I knelt down on the dusty ground beside her.

"So here I am Nani and I'm not dead."

We held onto each other as if our life depended on it. Father coaxed us to our feet and the three of us stood cuddling and hugging, Nani stroking at my hair and talking to me gently, telling me everything would be fine. Her voice was like a melody to me, the sweetest voice in the world for sure.

"I'm sorry Nani. I'm sorry for smelling so bad."

It came to me that I hadn't been showered for several days.

"I stink Nani. I'm sorry."

My mother was wiping away my tears with her fingers as she laughed and said that whatever daughters smelled like it was never unpleasant. She said I was her creation, her flesh and blood and then she led me into the house. It was exactly the same as I remembered it and I was surprised how warm it felt. I asked my mother what month it was and she said it was the end of July. The sun had baked into the stone for a couple of months now and it felt so comfortable. She led me through the lounge and towards the stairs. She said she was taking me to the bathroom and would wash me. Agi followed behind.

We stood in the bathroom as she started to fill the bath. When she began to undress me Agi made some excuse and went to leave the room. I asked him not to go, what did I care if my father saw me naked after everything I'd been through? But Agi was Agi and he just wouldn't do it and he left. My mother stripped me and helped me into the hot water.

She took an age to bathe me, soaping me all over and then rinsing the bubbles off with the showerhead. She repeated the exercise at least four or five times kissing me all over and telling me how much she'd missed me and that I would always be the most important person in the world to her, no matter what happened.

At last, she lifted me out and towelled me dry with a big soft fluffy towel. And as I stood motionless like a three-year old child she dressed me in clean clothes. My clean clothes, even though they were now two or three sizes too big. And still, I shivered and I didn't know why because I had the sun on my bones and the water in the bath and the shower had been hot, almost too hot and my parents were with me and I couldn't understand it.

"I'm cold Nani."

"It's normal loçki, you're tired and you're hungry, that's why you tremble. Your Nani will make it all right."

She left the bathroom and came back a couple of minutes later. She wrapped a big blanket around me and led me back downstairs. She made me lie on the sofa and sat down there with me smiling. She reached for the TV remote control and switched it on. She was flicking through the channels clearly looking for something specific. And then she found it. A Tom and Jerry cartoon and she stoked my hair as she said.

"Your favourite. Everything's all right now."

It had been many years since I had watched Tom and Jerry but she was right, it was my favourite and for several blissful minutes I forgot about everything I had been through as the little mouse tormented the cat and every now and again poor Tom got his comeuppance from the big bulldog. Tom and Jerry, if only life was that simple.

Mum was inspecting my bruises and muttering to herself, cursing under her breath and when she saw the scar on my calf muscle she started to cry again.

"Please don't cry Nani," I said, "it's nothing. I have only a few hours with you so please don't cry, we haven't time for that sort of thing."

She cradled my head in her arms and told me to sleep for a while, told me that when I woke there would be a feast waiting for me like I'd never seen before. With the beautiful bouquet of my dear Nani all around I fell asleep almost immediately.

I dreamt, but I dreamt I was back in the cell. It had prayed on my mind the deal that I'd heard the guards discuss with my father. It was just for one night they'd said and my father had agreed. *It's a deal*, he'd said but I didn't want to go back there again. The two guards were chasing me along the corridor and the corridor went on forever. It was never ending and I ran and ran and yet they couldn't catch me no matter how hard they tried. I ran to the point where I collapsed through exhaustion. It seemed so vivid, so real.

When I awoke I was still half asleep and didn't know where I was. It felt different and instinctively I stretched my legs. Something was strange, there was no contact with any wall. For six months I had slept twisted, unable to stretch out fully. My head was resting against something soft. Where was I? I opened my eyes wide and looked into my mother's tear- stained eyes. She sat in the same position she had been sitting in when I fell asleep and she continued to stroke my hair.

"I'm home?" I asked puzzled.

"You're home ciki." she replied.

It was beginning to turn dark outside, the sun was slowly disappearing and I was angry with myself because I knew I only had one night with my parents and I had surely wasted many hours.

"How long have I slept?" I asked.

My mother ignored the question and asked if I was hungry.

"Yes. I am starving."

"Is she up?" my father called from the kitchen.

She eased herself from the chair at the same time calling for my father who replaced her on the sofa as she made her way to the kitchen. It was Agi's turn to hold and caress me as my mother busied herself in the kitchen.

My father was laughing as he spoke.

"You've no idea how much food she has prepared in there."

I could smell it. The delicious aroma drifting in from the kitchen took me back in time, to my childhood, to a time the world was at peace, where we didn't have a care in the world. I dozed on and off on my father's knee until my mother announced the first dish was ready. She walked towards me with three small bowls on a tray as the steam rose towards the ceiling.

"Here you are loçki," she said.

"What is it Nani?"

"Bean broth."

I burst out laughing and by the look of disappointment on my face, my mother sensed something was wrong.

"What is it?"

"Oh Nani, you don't know how much bean broth I have had forced down me in the last six months. Every day they brought me bean broth, sometimes I ate it for breakfast and supper too and if I didn't see another bowl of bean broth for the rest of my life it wouldn't worry me."

My mother started to protest, instinctively defending her cooking and saying how much better her bean broth was than the bean broth from a Serbian soldier's kitchen.

Father would have none of it.

"Take the bean broth away and bring the girl something else. You have enough food to feed ten armies."

Father wasn't wrong. My mother brought me a tray and I sat up on the sofa while they brought in the food. We started with a plate of Suxhuk, those delicious Turkish-style sausages. I swear they were the nicest things that had ever passed my lips as the spicy flavours danced around my mouth. My mother and father sat on the floor watching me eat as they nibbled on a plate of Suxhuk between them. I hadn't even finished before Nani was on her feet and back in the kitchen. My father brought a small coffee table and placed it in front of the sofa and in came the meat and potato pastry pie, the Pite. It looked like the size of a car wheel. I couldn't help laughing and then as soon as she had placed the plate on the table she was back in the kitchen and returned with a dish of Sarma and another dish of rice and chicken.

"Nani," I said, "how much do you think I can eat?

She shrugged her shoulders and frowned.

"You tell me you haven't eaten for six months and I can see that from the way the flesh hangs from your bones that it's probably true."

It was true. I looked like something from Auschwitz in those black-and-white news footage videos from Nazi Germany but the harsh reality was that my stomach had shrunk and after eating the Suxhuk I was starting to struggle and the sight of so much food was even making me slightly nauseous. But Agi brought me some tea and I sipped at it and it helped to wash things down and I made sure I had a little something of everything. They had brought in a plate of sliced tomatoes, lightly salted. I had forgotten what fresh fruit and vegetables tasted like. The simple but exquisite taste of the tomatoes exploded onto my taste buds at the back of my mouth. I felt alive again. I bit gently into the flesh and the waterfall of flavour surged around my mouth. I was truly mesmerised and remember looking down at my parents who had appreciated my reaction to something so simple.

We sat like that for hours, a forkful of Sarma then a tiny slice of tomato, a piece of Pite and some rice and chicken. I ate until I felt my stomach would surely burst, I ate until my stomach begged me to stop feeding it. We drank a little tea outside and watched as the sun disappeared completely behind the mountain. It was so peaceful as I sat on my father's knee. I listened to the sounds of the night creatures as they began to stir and Nani sat behind me stroking my hair, every now and again kissing me.

I began thinking what it would be like to sleep in a normal bed, on a soft mattress - my mattress and the fact that I would have to go back with the Serbian soldiers the following day didn't particularly bother me because I knew this was a significant development and I dared to hope. Things can change I told myself, don't worry, put your trust in God. I tried to think of the good people in the world, my parents, Uncle Demir for example and convinced myself that the evil men like Kupi and my Serbian tormentors would always be outnumbered, always ultimately be defeated. They might win an odd skirmish or a battle, but they would never win the war against innocent civilians. I would always believe in good over evil and sitting there looking up at the backdrop of our beautiful silhouetted mountain with the greatest parents anyone could ever hope for reinforced my determination and I almost began to believe it.

We went back inside and my mother served up a sweet plate of Baklava. I managed to eat half of it then she brought a plate of tatlia, thick biscuits soaked and cooked in syrup. How I ate two I'll never know.

"No more Nani," I pleaded, "just let me go to my room I have missed it so much. I want to lie on my mattress and sleep forever, I want the rays of the sun to wake me tomorrow morning and I want to wake up free even if it's just for one day."

My father was back sitting on the floor staring up at me and I noticed that his bottom lip was trembling.

Something was wrong. Suddenly the warmth I had enjoyed for so many hours turned to ice.

CHAPTER TWENTY-FIVE
NEWS I SIMPLY COULD NOT COMPREHEND

"Talk to me Agi. What is it?"

My father was crying.

"I'm sorry loçki but you won't be sleeping here tonight."

The bowl of Baklava I had been holding fell to the floor.

"What?"

"Do you think I'm going to send you back there?" he said, "what sort of father do you think I am?"

I was speechless at first. I couldn't bear the thought of not spending a night in my old bed. My father was full of apologies but told me he had planned my escape for several weeks and it had taken him many months to get the money together for my release.

"It's all about the money," he said. "The spying charges were nonsense, I'd be surprised if they questioned you more than once or twice. War creates murderers and profiteers. Wherever there is conflict, you'll find a man ready to torture, rape and kill in the name of the cause, and to line his pocket with a quick easy buck."

I could hardly speak. Agi had it spot on, it was always about the money and it had been the same with Kupi. Men play-acting as soldiers pretending they had a just reason and all along they were lining their own pockets, parading in the streets as heroes and freedom fighters. What was it Brian had once said to my father?

War is undertaken for the acquisition of wealth. There are no exceptions.

Agi was on his knees by the sofa as I found my voice.

"I'm not going Agi, I'm staying here and I'm going to bed."

He was shaking his head. He reached for my hands and held them tight,

"I can hardly walk," I said, "how do you expect me to escape and run again? I was strong when you sent me to Pristina, but look at me now."

He wasn't listening.

"I have organised your escape. You are going to your uncle in England."

"I can't do this Agi, I won't do it."

My mother sat on the sofa beside me. "Listen to your father Lurata."

I was beginning to get angry with them. This wasn't what it was supposed to be like. I wanted to climb the stairs to my room and take a wash in my bathroom with the smell of soap I had been familiar with. Then change into those soft pyjamas that were under the pillow, climb under the duvet, pull it up to my chin and sigh as the warmth of the duck feathers enveloped me. Within minutes I'd be in another land, a different place, an altogether beautiful place that no one could stop me from going to. It had been almost magical up to now, why had they spoiled it? I turned towards my father.

"Then we can do it in the morning."

"We can't," he said. "The soldiers will come and ..."

He didn't finish the sentence and I realised what he was saying. I looked at him and then to Nani, and then back to him.

"You're not coming with me?"

He shook his head.

"I won't go without you."

I cried harder than I ever had, I was almost hysterical as I lay back on the sofa and covered my eyes with my hands.

I was praying with my hands clasped together.

"I wanted one night with them, just one night dear God, one night in my own bed and I prayed and I asked you for that and you've let me down, you've let me down again. Why do you do this to me?"

My father was getting agitated.

"We will need to go in thirty minutes."

Still, I argued and protested and asked him why they couldn't come with me. He said something about the money, said that it was impossible. I always listened to my father as he had a way with words and was always very persuasive but I was fighting him like I'd never fought him before. My mother was sitting on the floor packing a bag for me and then it hit me like a blow from a sledgehammer, a thought far worse than anything I had been through, a vision a thousand times worse than any torture I had ever gone through.

My lip was trembling and I began to cry as I blurted out the words.

"But they'll kill you."

My mother looked down at the bag and threw a few more things in as my father stood and walked back through to the kitchen ignoring me. I knew what these men were like and my father had brokered a deal. They would be furious if they found I'd fled.

I almost threw myself from the sofa and ran through to the kitchen.

"I won't go. They'll kill you."

Father was standing by the sink washing a cup or a dish with his back to me. He turned slowly.

"I know they'll kill us so you had better say goodbye to your Mother."

He held out his hands and I ran to him burying my face in his chest.

"This will be the last time you'll see us," he whispered before kissing the top of my head.

I argued with my father right up until the time I left the house but I was wasting my time. I told my parents that life would not be worth living without them but they would not listen. They were sacrificing their own lives to save mine and at that point, I realised how much I meant to them. This was a love that no words could begin to describe and it was so powerful to me that I found a determination from somewhere, a determination that told me I had to win this final battle. If that's what my parents truly wanted then I would make it to

England and I would survive and I would beat my tormentors otherwise their sacrifice would have meant nothing.

I told my mother she was the best friend a daughter could ever wish to have and we held each other for so long. Agi kept telling me that we had to leave. When I eventually let go of my mother she collapsed onto the ground in the garden and she put her hands together and looked skywards.

"Dear God, why have you punished us so much?" she said as the tears stained the ground.

I asked myself the same question.

It was pitch black as we made our way across the fields at the front of the house. I remember it being very flat and the moon was bright with millions of stars lighting our path through the short grass. I could hear the sound of the wild dogs barking in the distance, the dogs with no owners who lived in the mountains.

In due course we crossed the main motorway, thankfully it was almost deserted and then after a twenty-minute walk we crossed the main Serbia to Macedonia road. Agi led me a little further and we walked close to a river and up ahead on the road I could make out the shape of a truck despite the blackness of the night. The main lights were out and I could see the faint glow of the parking lights.

Father stopped.

"Wait there."

He walked around the truck and disappeared from view, coming back just a couple of minutes later.

"I need to put you in the truck now," he said.

I wrapped my arms around him and ran my hands through his thick hair.

"I love you Agi, I will make you so proud of me."

He was kissing me and crying, telling me he couldn't be more proud of me as it was.

"You are the best daughter a father could ever have hoped for."

"You are not going to die Agi, I know it."

"Perhaps not," he said, "but we will always be there with you loçki. If you think of us hard enough we will always be there with you. Promise me you will remember that."

"I will Agi, I will."

He walked me to the passenger seat of the truck and opened the door for me. He hugged and kissed me one last time. He smelled of Agi, my beautiful Agi and I knew that the smell would never leave me no matter what. As the truck pulled away, I looked in the side mirror for one last look at my father but it was too dark and I couldn't see him and I felt somehow as if I had been cheated.

I could see the lights of Veliki Trnovac over to the west and I watched carefully as they gradually disappeared from view. I had never felt so alone in the world, I felt like an orphan with no roots. I remembered my father's final words. I closed my eyes tight and within a few seconds, my beautiful parents were with me once again.

Agi had been right.

THE END

EPILOGUE

In 1991 Lurata was just eleven years old when her home country of Yugoslavia started to disintegrate into chaos as a result of disorder in several autonomous regions. Groups, mobs, self-proclaimed and elected leaders as well as individuals paraded under the flags of nationalism and sought independence from Yugoslavia, which prompted the president to send armed security forces to the regions affected, initially Bosnia and Hercegovina.

On 25th June 1991, Slovenia and Croatia declared their independence from Yugoslavia, which resulted in more troops being sent to secure international borders. The problem across the entire Slavic states and autonomous regions was perfectly demonstrated in Bosnia and Hercegovina where the population was made up of Bosniaks, Serbs, Croats, Yugoslavs, Montenegrins and Albanians. The region was also diverse in religious practices with Orthodox Christians, Catholics and Muslims all practising and preaching that their particular religion was God's chosen one.

It was a recipe for disaster, which was exactly what happened. Like the vast majority of the population in the land known as the former Yugoslavia, Lurata Lyon had a mixture of blood flowing through her veins. With Turkish grandparents and Yugoslavian parents as well as links to Macedonia, Albania and Serbia, there were times she could be forgiven for not knowing who was fighting who or indeed which side she actually belonged to. It was the same right across Yugoslavia, from Slovenia and Croatia in the north to Kosovo and Macedonia in the south.

During the mid-nineties the conflict spiralled out of control, which prompted the UN, NATO and the EC to take a hand and diplomatic solutions such as The Vance Owen peace plan were unveiled to the waiting world. The agreements appeared to achieve little as large-   scale fighting broke out between Bosniaks and Bosnian Croats and the Markale Market in Sarajevo was mortared in February 1994 in a scene reminiscent of Guernica at the beginning of The Spanish Civil War. It was also in early 1994 that NATO war-planes first conducted air strikes in the region.

In 1995 Lurata and her family heard about the horrendous massacre in Srebrenica where 7000 Muslim men were massacred and in the following year the war came dangerously close to her home town of Veliki Trnovac as the Kosovo Liberation Army declared open hostility towards Serbia and in particular soldiers of the Serb Army.

After the near massacre of Lurata's home town towards the end of the war in Kosovo her father took the heart-wrenching decision to send her to Pristina, the capital of Kosovo believing hostilities there were almost over and that NATO troops were in control of the peaceful city streets.

Lurata was caught up in the aftermath of the Kosovo war, a war that claimed nearly 12000 deaths with another 4000 reported missing and unaccounted for some twelve months after the hostilities ceased.

When Lurata arrived in Pristina an estimated 800,000 Kosovo Albanians were either displaced, unaccounted for, or had simply fled their homes. According to the Yugoslav Red Cross 200,000 Serbian refugees had also left the country to escape anti-Serb attacks and riots.

It was the perfect formula for the would-be criminals and lawless gangs to step in and make a killing, where not only life was cheap, it was almost impossible to identify a murder from an accident, an execution from a genuine casualty of war. As one leading war prosecutor described - "It was one vast crime scene."

Azem Kupi disappeared from the radar after Lurata's ill-fated return to Veliki Trnovac preferring to keep a low profile but his name cropped up again and again with people accusing him of many crimes perpetrated during the course of the conflict. There were many accusations levelled against him from residents of the town of Kukes in North-eastern Albania where in his role as a commander of the KLA, he allegedly mistreated and tortured ethnic Albanian prisoners at the detention facility there. But altogether more sinister accusations were being levelled at Kupi relating to a concentration camp in Daphne in Drenica, where it was said he participated in the executions and torture of prisoners and removed their organs where he sold them on the black market for up to $40,000 at a time.

Azem Kupi was not arrested until October 2000 and it was only by a stroke of luck that he was. He was detained by the UN Mission in Kosovo, following a shooting incident at one of Pristina's nightclubs after which he was charged with involvement in organized crime networks and extortion under the pretence of financing KLA activities.

Kupi was tried in April 2001, and sentenced to 5 years and 6 months in jail by the UNMIK Tribunal for endangering security and damaging the property of others through extortion.

In 2002 the EU Rule of Law Mission (EULEX) began an investigation into Kupi for mistreatment of persons held in KLA facilities during the conflict.

It was not until the summer of 2011 that Kupi was found guilty of committing war crimes against civilians and sentenced to 15 years in prison by the Mitrovica district court. Three accomplices were also found guilty of torturing civilians to obtain information and confessions. In court, it was revealed that Kupi was a close associate of the Prime Minister during the war which showed just how far Kupi's influence over the region stretched.

There are many who say that Kupi escaped lightly after the 2011 conviction and that his worst atrocities were never detailed during either trial. Several thousand people remain missing in Kosovo, a country that José Pablo Baraybar, a Peruvian who headed the U.N.'s Office on Missing Persons described as "one of the most exhumed places on earth."

An American journalist Michael Montgomery began amassing troubling stories involving the K.L.A. claiming multiple sources told him that, in the days after Milosevic's defeat, the K.L.A. had shipped accused traitors to camps in Albania. A former K.L.A. driver said that he had been given orders not to hurt anyone. Once his captives were in Albania, they were taken to a house where doctors were present. The driver heard that the doctors sampled the prisoners' blood and assessed their health. Several sources implied that this caretaking had a sinister purpose. The K.L.A. was harvesting the prisoners' organs and selling them on the black market.

He sent a memo to the U.N.'s missing persons office in Kosovo, asserting that, in 1999 and 2000, between one hundred and three hundred prisoners were taken to Albania where some were dispatched to a makeshift clinic that extracted body organs from the captives. The U.N. forwarded the memo to the International Criminal Tribunal for the former Yugoslavia, or I.C.T.Y. The tribunal, established in The Hague in 1993, was designed to bring a measure of justice to those who had suffered horrors in the Balkans.

As the years passed there was never any shortage of accusations and official investigations and reports in which organ harvesting and the name of Azem Kupi were strongly linked.

Former K.L.A. officials had long denied the existence of detention camps in Albania, but the Kupi trial proved otherwise and marked one of the most prominent convictions to date of a K.L.A. leader. The judges rendered their verdict after sixteen witnesses, most of them former captives, testified to scenes of depravity. One Kosovo Albanian testified about being detained in Kukes, along with his brother. They had been accused of being spies - charges that they denied. One night, the guards took the two brothers into an interrogation room and made the two brothers watch as guards beat another prisoner, clubbed him with a rubber-wrapped baseball bat, and rubbed salt into his wounds. Kupi himself beat the prisoner with a crutch and then ordered his men to beat one brother with metal bars. He repeatedly lost consciousness and they tortured him further by dunking his head in water. On another occasion, the guards at Kukes fitted him and his brother into bulletproof jackets and fired Kalashnikovs at their stomachs until they collapsed. Later, a guard shot one brother in the knee. His sibling begged the guards for help, but his brother bled all night and died the next day.

What isn't in doubt is that Lurata Lyon had a lucky escape at the hands of Azem Kupi. His power and influence and downright ruthlessness and barbarity made him a formidable opponent. Just to survive her captivity was a minor miracle, to escape and find it within herself to pen this remarkable book is testimony to her fortitude and courage.

The Serbian soldiers who held Lurata captive for six months have not been identified or held to account.